PREACHING THE
TOPICAL SERMON

Also by Ronald J. Allen
(with Clark M. Williamson)

The Teaching Minister

────────────

PREACHING THE TOPICAL SERMON

Ronald J. Allen

WESTMINSTER/JOHN KNOX PRESS
Louisville, Kentucky

To
Moriah
Our Second Daughter
Whose Name Bespeaks Our Trust
That God Is Faithful
To Her
And to Her World
Even as on the Mountain
Long Ago

Book design by Publishers' WorkGroup

First edition

Published by Westminster/John Knox Press
Louisville, Kentucky

This book is printed on acid-free paper that meets the American National Standards Institute Z39.48 standard.♾

PRINTED IN THE UNITED STATES OF AMERICA

2 4 6 8 9 7 5 3 1

Library of Congress Cataloging-in-Publication Data

Allen, Ronald J. (Ronald James), 1949–
    Preaching the topical sermon / Ronald J. Allen—1st ed.
        p.   cm.
    ISBN 0-664-25306-7

    1. Topical preaching.   I. Title.
BV4235.T65A44   1992
251—dc20   91-45553

CONTENTS

PREFACE

PERHAPS YOU, AS A PASTOR, HAVE HAD AN EXPERIENCE LIKE THIS. The phone rings in the kitchen on Saturday afternoon. A couple from the congregation, both over eighty years of age, have been found dead in their apartment. Bill tied a plastic bag over Betty's head. Then Bill put his old hunting rifle into his mouth and took his own life.

You make pastoral calls. You contact the couple's children who live far away, expressing concern and establishing a time and place to meet when they arrive in town. You notify the elder who leads the congregation's bereavement ministries. You visit the brother and sisters who live in town and you briefly stop by the homes of Bill and Betty's best friends. Everywhere the mood is the same. "We can't believe it."

After supper, you sit at your desk to look at the sermon you had prepared for Sunday when the phone starts to ring. Members of the congregation call to ask, "Have you heard?" and to express their dismay, shock, sorrow.

You think about Bill and Betty. Over twenty-five years ago, Betty was diagnosed with a degenerative disease. During the last several years, she was almost immobile. Bill had to lift her from bed, put her in a wheelchair, feed her, hold the phone to her ear for conversations. That grew more complicated as her body became so tender that she cringed at the slightest touch.

Bill had been a mechanic. Although he did not make a large salary, careful management had made it possible for them to have a secure and pleasant (if modest) life while he was working. But their retirement income had not kept up with inflation, especially their rising medical costs. The quality of their life-style eroded, and Bill's self-esteem with it. Bill had grown weaker and less able to take care of Betty. Then, a few weeks ago he had returned from the doctor's office with bad news: cancer. The doctor proposed to treat it with a massive program of radiation and chemotherapy but was pessimistic about long-term prospects.

These things lie in your heart as you pick up the manuscript of your sermon for Sunday. The text is the story of John the Baptist in Matthew 3:1–12. You focused on Matthew's admonition, "Bear fruit that befits repentance . . ." and you had sharpened the sermon with a prophetic edge. However, a slashing call for repentance hardly seems appropriate now.

But what do you preach, especially since you will preach only fourteen hours from now? You think about the possibility of another biblical text. But you grew up in the church at a time when the Bible was not strongly emphasized in the educational program or in your pastor's preaching. Your family did not read the Bible at home. Your seminary courses in Bible focused more on methods of critical biblical interpretation than on the content of the Bible itself. In fact, the embarrassing truth is that you have not read the whole Bible. The use of a lectionary is improving your familiarity with scripture, but the Bible is still not "in your bones."

Your next impulse is to turn to Romans 8:39 (nothing, "in all creation, will be able to separate us from the love of God in Christ Jesus our Lord"). As you mull over the passage, you realize that you may want to refer to this theme but that you use this passage so often in your preaching that to turn to it now feels tired and almost hackneyed.

Finally, given the delicacy of the situation, the nearness of the sermon, and your inability to feel at home in a biblical text, you decide to speak on the basis of the gospel message alone. In a sense, the gospel itself becomes the "text" of the sermon.

You work on the sermon, articulating the congregation's thoughts and feelings, recalling Bill and Betty, thinking about issues relative to health care and the elderly, puzzling over the poignant ethical concerns raised by the circumstances of the deaths. You bring it all into the presence of gospel. You remember voices from scripture that are expressive and instructive. You recollect pertinent themes from systematic theology. You know the sermon is not group therapy, but you see points at which your background in pastoral counseling can help you preach. You do not try to deal with the full range of ethical issues in this sermon, but you make notes for future reference.

On the one hand, you sense that you are taking an appropriate route. You are bringing good news from God to a difficult situation. On the other hand, you feel a little guilty because your homiletics professors and textbooks exclusively emphasized biblical (or "expository") preaching. You feel as though you are not quite *preaching* because you are not working systematically through a biblical text.

You may not know it, but you are preparing a topical sermon. You move not from text to sermon but from a topic (the painful death in the nexus of congregational life) to a consideration of the topic in the light of the gospel without centering it in the exposition of a biblical text.

This book commends self-conscious, disciplined, theologically mature topical preaching as an occasional alternative to the biblical sermon. Topical preaching is not a new idea. Honorable sermons with a topical character have been a part of the church's life since its early years. As recently as the middle of the twentieth century, topical preaching received positive attention in preaching textbooks and was practiced widely in local pulpits. (For representative earlier treatments of topical preaching, see Appendix A.)

Of course, the topical preaching of the preceding generation was widely criticized as theologically vacuous. However, malpractice does not mean that topical preaching is itself malefaction. Suppose a patient with a broken right foot comes to a physician. In the haste of treatment, the physician mistakenly takes an x-ray of the patient's left foot. The x-ray equipment is quite functional, even though the physician took a film of the wrong foot. But when the machine is aimed at the right foot, the physician gets the right picture. Similarly, when the methods of topical preaching are focused in a theologically credible way, the topical sermon can be a credible instrument of witness.[1]

As far as I know, David Buttrick's epic *Homiletic* offers the only genuinely contemporary model for topical preaching.[2] Buttrick does not use the designation "topical preaching." In fact, he seems studiously to avoid it (perhaps to distance his approach from the thin topical preaching of earlier years). Still, his "preaching in the mode of praxis" is similar to what we often (and here) refer to as topical preaching. *Homiletic* has rightly claimed the interest of the homiletics community. But, strangely, Buttrick's "preaching in the mode of praxis" has drawn almost no attention.

The present work is a modest attempt to join Buttrick in exploring an important, if occasional, form of preaching today. Chapter 1 lays out a map of current homiletical terrain so that we can locate the nature and purpose of the topical sermon. Chapter 2 discusses occasions when the topical sermon is appropriate. Chapter 3 presents a method for preparing the topical sermon. Chapter 4 suggests several forms that the preacher might use when developing a topical sermon. Chapter 5 offers strategies for preaching on controversial subjects.

Chapter 6 is composed of topical sermons that were preached to congregations by pastors and that illustrate different approaches to topical preaching.

This preface gives me the opportunity to make a public record of my indebtedness to Professor Buttrick's impressive work. I also wish to thank Richard Lancaster, an exquisite preacher and formerly my partner in the homiletics classroom at Christian Theological Seminary, Indianapolis, for several excellent suggestions. And, of course, I thank my spouse and children for encouragement and support. Our household, which grew from six to seven during the preparation of this manuscript, is the source of a seemingly infinite number of topics of the kind discussed in this book.

CHAPTER ONE

LOCATING
THE TOPICAL SERMON
ON THE HOMILETICAL MAP

A GOOD MAP IS INVALUABLE WHEN PLANNING A LONG TRIP. IT lets you see your destination and gives you the possible routes for getting there. If you have a leisurely spring afternoon to get to a vacation cabin, you might be interested in scenic, slow, country roads. But if your aged parent has just had a stroke in a distant city, you want to take an interstate highway.

When the trip is unfamiliar, the map helps you know what to expect and how to prepare for the trip. If we are crossing the New Mexico desert in the middle of an August afternoon, I make sure that the air conditioner is working and that we have a jug of cool water in the car. But if we cross the Rocky Mountains in January, I pack thermal underwear, blankets, food, a shovel, and a flare.

If we get lost on the trip itself, a map can help us become reoriented. I know for a fact that an old Boy Scout can think he is going north to Indianapolis when he is actually going south to Nashville and only the combination of road signs and a map can convince him otherwise.

In much the same way, a map of the homiletical terrain can help us preachers know where we want to go in a given sermon. Such a map can let us see the choices of routes the sermon may take and can help us assess the advantages and disadvantages of each route so that we can consciously choose the path that seems most promising in light of our goals, needs, and the conditions of the time. A map can orient us as to what to expect during the journey and can help us plan what to take and what to leave behind. And if we get lost in the process of preparing or preaching the sermon, a map can alert us to landmarks that can get us back to the main road.

To use current theological vernacular, a map of contemporary homiletical theory and practice can help us become more critical of our preaching.[1] It can help us evaluate what we are trying to do in a given sermon, why we are trying to do it, and the appropriateness of our efforts. A useful map can help us clarify and assess our preaching and thus strengthen the preaching of the gospel.

The coordinates of the homiletical map

The edges of a good map contain coordinates that enable the traveler to locate places on the map. The homiletical map contains two sets of coordinates: those which locate a sermon on the basis of the content of the sermon; those which locate a sermon according to the pattern of arrangement with which a sermon is developed. (For representative attempts to classify sermons, see Appendix B.)

The content of a sermon is typically either expository or topical. The expository sermon originates in the exposition of a biblical text or theme. The text is a window through which to look at the gospel in relationship to the congregation. The biblical sermon shows how the ancient witness can enhance our sensitivity to God's presence, power, and purposes in the present. The exposition of the text will typically lead the preacher to interpret a contemporary need, issue, or situation in light of the gospel through the encounter with the text. (See Appendix C for basic guides to interpreting the Bible for expository preaching.)

2

Both types of sermons share a common purpose: to help the listeners discover the gospel in their world. But the two types of sermons approach this task by different routes.

The pattern of arrangement that is employed in the overall development of a sermon is typically either deductive or inductive. In the deductive sermon, the preacher makes the "big point" at the beginning of the sermon and then develops the point. Inductive movement begins with particular details and moves to the "big point."

When the possibilities of content and pattern of arrangement are combined, we may speak of four general types of sermons:

1. The expository-deductive sermon
2. The expository-inductive sermon
3. The topical-deductive sermon
4. The topical-inductive sermon

These are not the only categories by which to understand sermons, but they do give the preacher an angle of vision along which to reflect on the purpose and design of the sermon. We focus here on the topical sermon.

The cartography of the topical sermon

The topical sermon interprets a topic in light of the gospel but without originating or centering in the exposition of a biblical text or theme. This, of course, raises a natural question: "What is a topic?" A topic is a need, an issue, or a situation which is important to the congregation (whether or not the congregation consciously recognizes its importance), which calls for interpretation from the perspective of the gospel, and which can be better addressed from the standpoint of the gospel itself than from the standpoint of the exposition of a particular passage (or passages) from the Bible.

The last clause is important. A topical sermon is designed

3

for those needs, issues, or situations which "can be better addressed. . . ." I join the great number of current homiletical witnesses in believing that the expository sermon is the life-blood of weekly parish preaching. The Bible helps sustain the church in generation after generation. We need only recall the names of Augustine, Luther, Calvin, Wesley, Campbell, and Barth to remember the revelations and reformations that can occur when the pages of scripture are opened appropriately.

However, the Bible is not the only guide for the Christian life. Furthermore, the Bible is silent on some subjects and can scarcely be used to address others (except by means of hermeneutical sleight of hand). Occasionally the Bible is not the best guide and, in some few instances, the Bible is actually an unreliable guide.[2]

As we shall see in chapter 2, there are unusual circumstances when the preaching of the gospel is well served by a topical sermon. I want to make it clear here that I am not selling biblical preaching for a mess of topical pottage. I do not propose that topical preaching replace expository preaching as the fundamental mode of pulpit discourse. Rather, the topical sermon is an occasional alternative to regular expository preaching. The topical sermon is a vitamin supplement to the nourishing fare of regular preaching from the Bible.

The preparation of the topical sermon moves in three stages. First, the preacher becomes aware of a topic and determines that the topic is a suitable subject for conversation with the congregation. Second, he or she analyzes the topic with a credible theological method and determines what to say about the topic. Third, the preacher then determines how to put the sermon together so that it has a chance to be of maximum help to the congregation. In short, the preacher decides to say something, what to say, and how to say it.

Topics can come from any arena of life. Some topics come to expression in the lives of individuals and families. For example, does the church have a rationale, particularly a distinctively Christian one, for not using (or using) illegal drugs?

Other topics derive from the Christian community itself. For example, in the emerging pluralistic world, what relationship can the church have with the synagogue and the mosque? Still other topics come from the larger social setting in which we live, such as what can the church contribute to our understanding of the human relationship with nature as the global family contemplates the possibility of ecocide?

Of course, the headings of individual, churchly, and corporate are arbitrary. As Buttrick says, "In consciousness, there is always a self-in-a-social-world and a social-world-within-the-self."[3]

The center of the topical sermon is the interpretation of the topic in light of the gospel. The gospel is the dipolar news that God unconditionally loves each and every created entity and that God unceasingly wills justice for each and every created entity.[4] The gospel offers a vision of what the world is (loved unconditionally) and what it can become (a place of justice). A key question is, "How does the gospel lead us to understand the topic?"

In addition to a clear vision of the gospel, the preacher will want to have a working knowledge of the Christian tradition. This includes familiarity with the Bible, with the development of the witness of the church, and with current theological reflection.

In order to interpret the topic in light of the gospel, the preacher needs to have a full-bodied understanding of the topic itself. Such an understanding is crucial. On the negative side, it is crucial so the preacher will avoid oversimplification, caricature, misrepresentation, and even (unintentional) lying. The shepherd does not want to mislead the sheep. On the positive side, an accurate grasp of the topic is crucial so the preacher can deal truthfully with the topic, can provide maximum help to the congregation as they seek to understand and respond to the topic, and can accurately represent the relationship of the gospel to the topic. The integrity of the sermon and of the witness of the church are on the line.

5

In order to be confident of having a realistic grasp of the topic, the preacher may need to turn to the wide-ranging resources, such as psychology, sociology, economics, political analysis, the natural sciences, and the arts, that help us interpret life in the world today. When preaching on topics related to economic recession, for instance, the preacher needs to understand such things as the dynamics of the economic order that lead to recession, the psychological and social effects of recession upon parishioners, and realistic options for people whose lives are disrupted by recession.

The preacher may also use the Bible in the topical sermon. The biblical text does not shape the topical sermon as it does the expository sermon. But the Bible may play other roles in the sermon, such as providing general theological illumination. In any case, whenever the Bible appears in the topical sermon, the preacher should honor its literary, historical, and theological contexts. Topical preaching is never a license for prooftexting or other abuse.

The preacher may have an adequate working knowledge of the topic when beginning to prepare the topical sermon. But often preachers will enhance the integrity of their treatment of the topic by acknowledging that they are not sufficiently informed to speak knowledgeably about the topic. Therefore, a current library card is one of the best friends of the topical preacher.

The amount of research necessary to support some topical sermons will sometimes exceed the one week's time available for sermon preparation in pastoral work. I may be angered by executives of the financial world who lead banks and other financial institutions into insolvency even while growing wealthy themselves, but if I want the sermon to be more than a scattershot attack upon greed, I need a better foundation than a couple of articles from *Newsweek* and my own sense of moral outrage. The topical sermon typically benefits from advance planning.

Preachers also need to be in touch with their own biases and feelings regarding the topic. If these are left unexamined, they may warp the preacher's presentation of the topic.

In one respect, the topical preacher faces a greater danger than does the expositor. In the expository sermon, the presence of the biblical text tends to remind the preacher to ground the sermon in a theological point of view. If the hermeneutical movement leads biblical preachers from the text to local political issues, the text tends to remind the preachers to interpret the issues in light of theological conviction and not simply to air their own political beliefs.

Without the built-in reminder of the text, the topical preacher may be tempted to regard critical theological analysis as only an option. Losing sight of theological norms, the topical sermon can become a pale version of articles that might appear in *Reader's Digest,* a newsletter for social workers, or *The Mother Earth News.* Such a sermon may provide something genuinely helpful to the listener. But it does not fulfill the purpose which is the raison d'être of the church, namely, to help the congregation name the world specifically in terms of the gospel.

Topics usually manifest themselves at two levels. The first and more obvious level is the immediate symptom the listeners encounter in day-to-day living. By way of illustration, many households today experience debilitating stress. "Presenting symptoms" include household members who are anxious, exhausted, short-tempered, noncommunicative. Households are habitations of conflict, substance abuse, and human abuse.

At another level, topics manifest from situations related to our larger life system. A topic results from more than the decisions and actions of individual persons. The values and practices of our culture help create the conditions that encourage the manifestation of the topic. Buttrick further sees that "every situational sermon will have to include some critical assessment of our human understanding."[5] We need to understand the topic in its immediate and larger settings from the perspective of the gospel. For example, we humanly and uncritically tend to regard tensions in the home as a problem with which individual households must learn to cope. Hence, the pastor may preach on "how to handle stress" and the congregation may offer a workshop on stress management. While these offerings may help develop coping mechanisms, they do not help the congregation confront the roots of the problem. Thus, Buttrick wisely urges us to reread the phenomenon of stress in light of larger cultural values and systems. These include the devaluation of women, the emergence of the insular family and the loss of contact with the extended family, the rise of the ideal of the autonomous self, growth in life-style expectations that require ever greater household income, and competitive pressures and the need to prove one's worth in all areas of life. Stress in the home is thus influenced profoundly by cultural forces and values that are contrary to the gospel.

Systematic analysis and theological rigor are two points that distinguish this enlarged approach to topical preaching from the topical preaching of the earlier years of our century. Buttrick points out that many earlier topical sermons had a simple twofold movement. They "begin with a description of a problem as humanly understood and, then, presto, the gospel is introduced as an answer or a solution or a cure." Buttrick continues, "If a sermon begins with human understanding of a situation, then, inevitably, the gospel will be expected to satisfy the situation as it is humanly understood."[6] The gospel becomes an Alka-Seltzer to calm our upset religious stomachs.

Ronald Sleeth, one of the most incisive and trenchant critics of earlier topical preaching, concluded that topical sermons often "departed into far countries, feeding on the husks of relevancy. This has resulted in topical preaching gone berserk."[7] Sleeth further laments that topical preachers have sometimes misrepresented the Bible and their own preaching by making reference to the Bible in the course of the sermon but without seriously relating the actual content of the text to the sermon.

In the worst instance, "this practice is really not using texts, but pretexts; it is running the text up the mast, or, to change the figure, jacking up the sermon and running a text under it."[8] This approach violates the integrity of the text, the preacher, and the sermon. However, as serious as these deficiencies are, they are not intrinsic to topical preaching.

Strengths of the topical sermon

While these qualities are not unique to topical preaching, they are characteristic of good topical preaching. Topical preaching of the revised type offers several strengths. The subject of the topical sermon is frequently drawn from things that are happening about the time the sermon is preached and that the congregation perceives as important. If the preacher has carefully chosen and focused the topic, and if the sermon approaches the topic so as to invite the listeners into a promising conversation, then from the very beginning the listener may think, "Ah, I want to pay attention to this." The preacher will not have to work hard to arouse interest in the topic. For example, in a congregation with a large group of single members, the preacher can usually assume a high degree of interest in a sermon on Christian sexual mores for the single life.

Of course, an imaginative preacher can help a congregation become interested in almost any subject, even what happened to the Jebusites. But frequently when the interest of the listener is already drawn in the direction of the sermon, the preacher can move easily and straightforwardly into the substance of the issue.

The congregation is often able immediately to connect the content of the topical sermon with their life experiences. A topical sermon on the Lord's Supper, for example, would usually be preached on the Sunday that the Lord's Supper is served. A good sermon enlarges the experience of receiving the bread and the cup.

The topical sermon teaches the congregation how to interpret life in the light of the gospel. To use current jargon, the topical sermon models theological method for the listeners. A topical sermon illustrates how to identify and describe a need, issue, or situation, how to reflect on that topic from the perspective of the gospel, and how to draw conclusions (and possible changes in perception and behavior) from the analysis.

Suppose the congregation hears a topical sermon focused on terrorism. The preacher describes acts of terrorism. The preacher laments the destructiveness of terrorist activities and the feelings of fear and revulsion that spread through the population when terrorist actions are reported. The preacher then asks, "What prompts a person to become a terrorist?" The answer is complex, but the preacher discovers a widespread theme in the self-description of terrorists. They are outraged about a particular injustice in the world and about the apparent indifference of decision makers to that injustice. They often perceive acts of dramatic violence as a way of last resort to win the attention of the world community. Of course, acts of terrorism must be condemned, and acts of terrorism do not always testify to the presence of genuine injustice. But, the preacher points out, when terrorism does result from genuine concern for an injustice, the answer to terrorism is more than rescuing the victims, punishing the terrorists, and installing metal and explosives detectors in all major airports. Brutality will continue until the injustice itself is rectified.

In the process of the sermon, the preacher leads the members of the congregation to identify their own perceptions and feelings on the topic, to probe beneath the surface manifestation of the topic to its systemic causes, and to consider alternatives that might help alleviate the problem. Perhaps the listeners can transfer this model to other situations. Suppose a neighbor down the street is exposed as a child molester. A member of the congregation might be able to think about the child molester in the systematic way that the preacher has modeled in the sermon. Thus, the person would be enabled to move beyond revulsion and fear to understanding and ministry.

Further, the last decade of the twentieth century is an opportune time for the preacher to use the topical sermon as a time to teach theological method in a direct way. People might benefit enormously from an occasional sermon that offers a practical method (perhaps even step by step) for thinking about personal and social issues.

I would like to emphasize that the topical sermon as I conceive it here does not establish a route for the sermon to travel every Sunday. But it does mark a useful place on the homiletical map.

Patterns of movement in the sermon

Where philosophers and logicians speak of deduction and induction with reference to tightly defined forms of reasoning, authors in the field of preaching think more generally of patterns of sermonic movement. Each pattern has its own strengths and weaknesses.[9]

Deductive reasoning moves from a general statement to a particular statement. In the deductive sermon, the preacher announces the big point of the sermon at the beginning and then develops the main point in particular ways. Fred Craddock and Locke Bowman suggest an upright triangle as a model of the process of deduction.[10] This is especially apt since the roots of the word *deduce* mean "to lead down." See Figure 1.

In a sense, the preacher hangs a theme banner between two telephone poles along the main street of the listener's consciousness and says, "Pay attention to this point as we ride together through this sermon."

The sermon can be developed in any number of ways. The preacher may draw out the implications of the general truth.

11

FIGURE 1

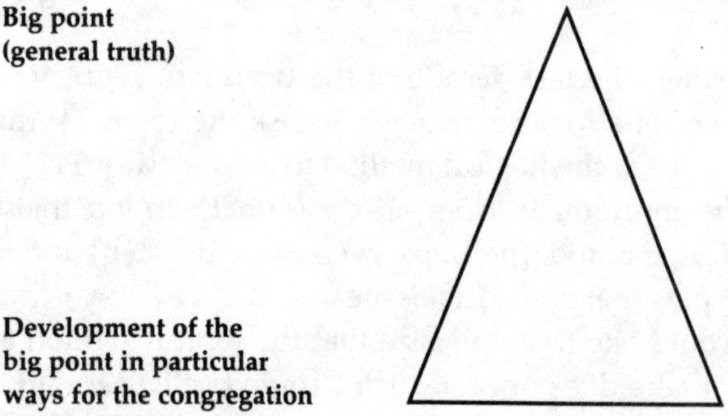

Big point
(general truth)

Development of the
big point in particular
ways for the congregation

The preacher may give examples that illustrate the major point and that relate the major point to the listeners. The preacher may defend the major claim. The preacher may apply the big idea to different spheres of life (such as the individual, the local community, the nation, the world). The preacher may enumerate points that follow from the major idea.

The great strength of the deductive approach is clarity. The listener has every opportunity to get the point. The deductive sermon also communicates a sense of security to the listener in that the listener catches the drift of the sermon right away and is not likely to be surprised by the content or development of the sermon. Further, the deductive sermon is very systematic. This allows the preacher to prepare the sermon in a very orderly way and it allows the listener to process the content of the sermon in an equally orderly way.

Deductive sermons are especially useful when the congregation is already generally sympathetic to the main premise and needs principally to have the preacher enlarge upon the premise and relate it to their experience.

Topical preachers will often find the deductive pattern useful when the sermon has the major function of explaining the Christian viewpoint in relationship to the topic. For instance, a deductive structure might help the preacher set forth the major tenets of a Christian doctrine. "Our denomination believes the following things concerning original sin. . . ."

A deductive structure is not as useful when the preacher wishes to challenge a view held by many members of the congregation. When the preacher announces a major premise that obviously disagrees with the assumptions of the congregation, listeners may be so alienated that they fail to hear the rest of the sermon.

Critics have exposed several deficiencies in the deductive sermon. Some charge that its structure is removed from life experience and that it does not allow for the complexity, ambiguity, and spontaneity of the real world. Life cannot be compressed into a preacher's syllogism or thesis. Thus, the very structure of the deductive sermon can bear false witness. Some point out that deduction is only secondarily the manner in which we typically come to discovery. When a child is left alone as it enters a new environment, the child learns about that environment by means of exploration. Others complain that the deductive sermon short-circuits the participation of the listener in the sermon. Someone once described the deductive sermon to me as predigested protein. The essential nutrients may be present, but the listener does not have the joy of eating the meal. Still others charge that the style of the deductive sermon evokes a hierarchicalism that works against the contemporary search for collegial modes of authority and the egalitarian mood of our time. Yet others lament that the deductive form has a tendency to lead to boring sermons. If you know the point in the first five minutes, why keep listening?

While such criticisms function as caution lights, they do not pose impassable roadblocks to deductive preaching. In the hands of a lively, sensitive communicator, the deductive sermon can bear a useful witness to the gospel.

Inductive reasoning moves from the particular to a general

FIGURE 2

Particulars that give
rise to the sermon

Development of resources
to make sense of particulars

Conclusion

conclusion. In the inductive sermon, the preacher moves from particular observations, questions, examples, experiences to a major conclusion that makes sense of the particulars. The word *inductive* comes from roots that mean "to lead into." This is an apt image. For the inductive preacher leads the hearer into the consciousness of aspects of life that call for interpretation and then moves to help the listener recognize clues in the Christian tradition that help lead to a faithful interpretation. Craddock and Bowman propose an inverted triangle as a visual model of the process of induction (see Figure 2).[11]

In a sense, the preacher says, "Look, here are some interesting things at this street corner of life. Come with me down this street while we explore them."

The inductive approach has been mentioned in homiletics textbooks for years. But since the publication of Craddock's landmark *As One Without Authority* in 1971, the compass of homiletical theory has been pointed toward the inductive approach. Many leading preachers and homiletics scholars operate out of an inductive paradigm even when they do not use the word *inductive* to describe their work.[12]

Proponents point out that life itself often has an inductive quality. Particular phenomena claim our attention and we pursue them to find out what they might mean to us. As noted earlier, inductive movement corresponds to the primary movement of human consciousness in the process of discovery. Furthermore, inductivity is now an integral part of our formal educational system as well as a significant component of the scientific method in which we are schooled.

The inductive sermon invites the participation of the listener in the sermon. In fact, Craddock compares the hearing of the inductive sermon to going on a journey.[13] The inductive sermon tends to be nonauthoritarian and frequently has a collegial quality, which makes it well suited for our time. Furthermore, the very structure of the inductive sermon can embrace the complexity, ambiguity, and spontaneity of the real world. By reserving the major point for the end, the inductive sermon maintains a certain suspense (rather like a short story), which sustains the listener's attention. And because the sermon often begins with matters that are close to their lives, the listeners can immediately sense the existential importance of the sermon.

Topical preachers will likely find that the inductive pattern is a reliable companion on the homiletical road. The inductive model is especially useful when preaching on controversial topics. The sermon eases the congregation into the topic, perhaps even developing empathy with aspects of the topic. The congregation is thus more receptive to entertaining new viewpoints. The topical preacher will also be attracted to an inductive arrangement when offering the listener an experience of the topic (a distinction from "making a point").

I strongly caution that the inductive sermon requires careful preparation. Unless the inductive sermon is well put together, the hearers may not get the point or enter appropriately into the experience of the sermon. (I have heard "inductive sermons" that turned out to be little more than streams of incoherent questions, stories, observations, and impressions.) And, the listeners may not need to go on a journey or make a fresh discovery on a given Sunday. Sometimes we need to have things explained as simply (and even as mechanically) as possible. For instance, writing this book is my first long-term experience using a computer. At first, I loved to learn how to use the computer by trial and error with a little help from the operator's manual. But now that I am into chapter 1, I want a quick, step-by-step explanation of how to make the computer work properly.

As noted earlier, preachers frequently, and to good effect, employ both patterns of arrangement in a single sermon. In the overall pattern of arrangement, a preacher may spend the first ten minutes in inductive development—raising an issue, analyzing it theologically, and coming to a conclusion. In the second ten minutes, the preacher may use the major conclusion as a premise that is applied deductively to the situation of the listeners. This results in a sermon that can be diagramed as an hourglass (see Figure 3).[14]

Within a sermon that generally follows one of the patterns of arrangement, a preacher may employ a movement that has the spirit of the other pattern of arrangement. For instance, in a generally inductive sermon, a preacher may make use of a deductive argument, perhaps even a syllogism.

The selection of a pattern for a particular sermon cannot be made by the author of a homiletics textbook. It can only be made by the critically thinking pastor who is well acquainted with the hearts, minds, behaviors, and biases of the members of the listening community.

Conclusion

This chapter has focused on the importance of ministers making critically informed decisions regarding the homiletical map we follow. Without meaning to undercut what I have said so far, I close with a caveat.

Experienced preachers frequently report that a sermon

FIGURE 3

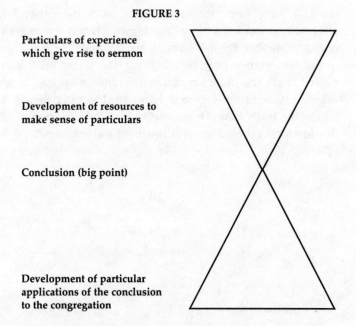

Particulars of experience
which give rise to sermon

Development of resources to
make sense of particulars

Conclusion (big point)

Development of particular
applications of the conclusion
to the congregation

takes on a life of its own in the process of preparation. The preacher may begin the journey to the pulpit with a clear idea of where the sermon is to go and how to get there. But the sermon changes as the preacher works. Unforeseen connections appear. Previously unnoticed paths beckon. The potholes on the planned roadway are worse than expected. A detour runs through a gorgeous valley that does not even appear on the map. Soon the sermon is on an alternate route.

This is quite natural and I do not want to discourage it. The preacher is not a fax machine whose mind conceives an idea and then transmits an exact reproduction of that idea to the mouth in one smooth impulse. The preacher is a creative being who responds to hunches, flashes of insight, accidents of discovery, free associations, intuitions, and the unexpected possibilities that emerge from disciplined research. Such diversions from the planned route often enhance the trip. Indeed, I have been so busy staring at a map that I have altogether missed the blooming dogwoods and redbuds in the countryside through which we were passing.

But, no matter how breathtaking the vistas on the unexpected road, the preacher will benefit from stepping back and asking, "Where am I going? How am I getting there? Am I taking the route that is most likely to help the sermon reach its destination in the minds and hearts of the listeners?"

CHAPTER TWO

OCCASIONS
FOR THE TOPICAL SERMON

A MINISTER MAY BECOME AWARE OF A TOPIC IN AS MANY WAYS as life has moments: in a conversation on the church parking lot after the elders' meeting, while watching the evening news, during a pastoral call, as a result of watching an insightful movie or reading a provocative volume of fiction, when hiking in the woods on vacation, or as a community-wide event bursts into public awareness. Some topics claim our attention in a flash while others dawn upon us as slowly as the fog lifts on a cloudy morning.

Given the occasional nature of the topical sermon, the preacher does not *search* for a subject for a topical sermon. A pastor needs only to let the windows of consciousness be open to the world. Needs, issues, and situations that are appropriate for topical preaching turn up in the course of living. This chapter considers eight representative circumstances when a topical sermon might offer a route to bring together the gospel and the congregation. Alert pastors will recognize other occasions for topical preaching.

But first a little backpedaling. A reader may think of expository sermons that fit each of the following situations. I claim neither that the expository sermon is impotent in these condi-

19

tions nor that the topical sermon is the only means by which to address them. Rather, I note that the topical sermon can serve the configurations of circumstances, needs, and issues that come to expression in these representative cases.

When time is short

Virtually all homiletical authorities recommend beginning sermon preparation well ahead of the date the sermon is to be preached. But things do happen late in the week which radically alter the listening climate and call for Christian interpretation: a tornado blows through town; a leading member of the community drops dead on a downtown sidewalk; an industrial accident threatens to turn the town's water supply into toxic waste; war breaks out in a place whose name you cannot even pronounce, much less locate on a map; a scientific discovery of dazzling promise bursts into the news.

In extreme moments, the preacher may be immediately swamped by a host of unanticipated pastoral responsibilities, such as calling on the bereaved or helping organize community action. But important as such roles are, the Sunday service is coming and one of the minister's most significant functions in extremity is to help the community begin to make Christian sense of the events. The sermon deserves the best attention that time allows.

Sometimes a pastor can salvage the text and insights from the sermon, which had already been prepared, and bring them to the new situation. But often, everything in the previous sermon, except the name of God, needs to be pushed off the road leading to the pulpit.

When preaching in a time of extremity, a preacher's first instinct is to pick up the Bible. We may, in fact, locate a text that helps interpret our situation. But where our great-grandparents would naturally (and almost unconsciously) begin to interpret an event in concert with the Bible, we must frequently enter the Bible through a concordance. Though we love the Bible, many of us do not have its fabric woven into our consciousness. When we draw upon the Bible, we must honor the exegetical and hermeneutical dimensions of a text. When time is short, we may not have time to do so carefully.

When time is short, I face a particular danger as I turn to the Bible. Feeling the growing magnetic pull of Sunday morning, I tend to grab the first word, verse, or passage suggesting even a distant relationship to the juncture in which I find myself. Lacking the time to explore the material exegetically and hermeneutically, I may use the material as little more than a prooftext. I may even misunderstand and misuse it. The listeners may not be permanently injured by this route, but if I would take another route, I could do them a better service. I could lessen the risk of misrepresenting the Bible (as well as the church and myself) and I could save time for more genuinely helpful sermon preparation activities.

The topical sermon is a practical, credible option when time is short and we are uncertain as to how to get into (or out of) the Bible. It provides the preacher with a way to bring the resources of the gospel directly into the life of the community.

When understanding or action is urgent

Even when the preacher has plenty of time for sermon preparation, the community may be gripped urgently and existentially by a need, issue, or situation. The topic is crucial, but we do not know quite what to make of it or how to respond to it. Buttrick identifies two such moments: when we face a crisis of understanding; when we face a crisis of decision.

In the crisis of understanding, our way of perceiving the order and purpose of life is thrown open. In the most dramatic instances, "Our world constructs are exposed as inadequate and a sense of finitude sweeps over us. In such moments, we question."[1] We are pressed against the limits of our understanding and we long for religion to fulfill one of its oldest and most important functions, to interpret the meaning of life.[2]

Crises of understanding may be tragic. A loaded school bus runs off a bridge and into a river. But some are positive. You hold your newborn in your arms for the first time. Some such moments are more social in character. A government commits an atrocity, traumatizing the nation. Other such moments are more personal. A twenty-eight-year-old woman with three preschool children is told she has less than six months to live.

In the crisis of decision, we must make an important choice. But, Buttrick says, "there are moments . . . when prereflective acting is impossible because impulses and conventions are in conflict, and postreflective precedents are simply not available. In such moments human beings agonize over decisions; they ask, 'What on earth am I to do?' "[3] We have no choice but to choose. But how?

Moments of decision come to individuals and to communities. When the United States and its allies began to bomb Iraq in 1991, many Christians had quickly to decide where they stood on the war and what to do about their position. Am I against military intervention? If so, what do I do? Do I send a telegram to my congressional representatives? Do I join the protests on the city square? Do I lie down across the gate of a military post? Do I refuse to pay the portion of my income taxes that go to military expenditures? Communities, too, must make significant choices. Refugees from Central America enter the United States illegally and make their way to our church building. Do we, as a congregation, give them sanctuary?

Of course, a biblical text may be an ideal frame for considering the need, issue, or situation. But questions of understanding and decision may rise within us with such intensity that they force other thoughts to the periphery of our minds. We can scarcely think of anything else and yet we do not know what to think. We need guidance that can help us organize and evaluate our thoughts and actions and that respects our freedom as decision makers.

In this environment, the preacher may decide to turn the full energy of the sermon to the topic alone. The pastor may conclude that giving an exposition of a biblical text or theme, in this exceptional case, would deflect time and attention that could better be given to clarifying our perception of the phenomenon that precipitated the crisis, to naming our feelings and thoughts, to identifying the factors that enter into understanding or decision making (especially the gospel and its norms), or to projecting the possible results of particular ways of thinking or acting.

A single homily will seldom replace the foundation, framing, finishing, and landscaping of a world construct. But a sermon whose edge is sharpened with the strop of the gospel can cut a significant swath in the debilitating underbrush in the mind and will of the congregation.

When the Bible is silent

The Bible does not comment directly on many needs, issues, and situations that confront the modern congregation and cry out for interpretation. This is not surprising given the differences between our world and the worlds of the Bible. It would not occur to a person living in a three-story universe to write a theological treatise on the ethics of creating a baby in a test tube.

Of course, even as I write I can hear readers objecting. The surprise is not how little the Bible speaks to the contemporary world but how much. Sensitive, disciplined hermeneutics can often bridge the gap between a biblical passage that appears to be wrapped in a shroud (or even sealed in a tomb) and modern lives, which are often measured by bytes on a computer.

But despite thoughtful biblical hermeneutics, some question marks continue to hang in the back of the Christian mind.

A topical sermon can bring these questions out of the dark and into the light where we can talk about them.

The existence of God is a clear example. The worlds of the Bible basically assumed the existence of God (and gods). In the Hellenistic era, for instance, the question was rarely "Do you believe in God?" The question was more likely "Which god do you serve?" The Bible deals extensively with the pernicious problems of polytheism and idolatry but little with God's existence as such.

Trust in God is the foundation of the Christian life. Yet it is not self-evident to today's person that there is a God in whom to trust. Everyday reality calls God's existence into question. How can we suffer the ravages of natural destruction and the monstrosities of moral evil and still believe in God? The person whose view of life awakened in a biology laboratory will not necessarily be led to posit the existence of God in order to account for all that is. People who do not recognize the phrase "acids of modernity" nonetheless feel the sting of those acids. A high school student asks, "How can I know there is a God?" After taking Introduction to Philosophy in college, the same student returns home to ask, "How can I know that I know there is or is not a God?" The preacher who takes Psalm 14 as a text ("The fool says in his heart, 'There is no God.'") and then berates unbelievers as stupid leaves little doubt as to the identity of the real fool.

A preacher cannot "prove" that God exists. As Craddock reminds us, no human being has walked all around God and taken pictures.[4] But, in the manner of Anselm's faith seeking understanding, the preacher can help the congregation understand why belief in God is reasonable in today's context. The classical arguments for God's existence (cosmological, teleological, moral, ontological) are not found in the Bible, but they might strengthen a congregation's confidence in God.

A topical sermon could provide a forum for a lively preacher to expose knotty questions about God's existence in language from the world of the congregation. The preacher could then unravel those questions[5] with the help of one of the classical arguments for God's existence. Indeed, it could be a challenging homiletical assignment to present the ontological argument in the language and imagery of a high-tech suburban community.

When the topic is larger than a single biblical text, image, or theme

Some topics, though discussed in the Bible, are larger than any single biblical passage, image, or theme. A responsible sermon needs to deal in a serious way with the cogent biblical material, but the scope of the church's reflection extends beyond the Bible.

This is particularly true of foundational Christian doctrines. The fundamental beliefs of Christian communions are typically rooted in the Bible. Specific biblical references are like the root system of a fruit tree. Below ground, the roots spread through the soil in a wide web. The root system provides the tree with essential nutrients. The roots are continuous with the tree, but when the tree breaks through the surface of the soil, it develops a trunk, leaves, and fruit. These latter mature, in part, because the sprout responds to sunlight, an important factor that is not in the soil. Photosynthesis is almost as important to the tree as water or the roots. The tree bears nourishing fruit when the combination of rainfall, temperature, and sunlight is right. While the roots are integral, the fruit is more than the roots.

Similarly, in the formation of Christian doctrine, the Bible is the root. As passages, images, and themes break through the surface of consciousness at later moments of history, the church reflects upon them in the light of the prevailing worldview. Mutual critical correlation (a kind of theological photosynthesis) takes place.[5] The witnesses of the Bible help shape the worldview of the church. But at the same time, the church brings the biblical testimony into categories of the church's own time and cultural epoch. In the process, the biblical testament is usually transformed into something more than it was. Christian doctrine emerges when these transformations are brought together in a systematic way. The preacher wants the sermon to be nourished by the Bible and supported by the trunk of the church's tradition, but the preacher particularly wants to pick the fruit of reflection.

Christology is an example. The meaning of the event of Jesus Christ is decisive for the identity and mission of the church. Therefore, from time to time, the minister will want to bring a sermon that goes beyond any single christological image (for example, Jesus as Son of God) and that speaks systematically and synthetically of what Jesus Christ means to the church in our contemporary context. The literature of earliest Christianity contains not one uniform Christology but several different images and ideas, which interpret the significance of the event of Jesus to particular communities and moments. To oversimplify, Paul focuses on Jesus as Lord. Mark sees Jesus as the apocalyptic Son of man. The fourth Gospel is oriented to Jesus as Word. Jesus is the pioneer and perfecter of the faith in Hebrews. The pluriform witnesses of the early church share a common underlying conviction that the event of Jesus Christ is a revelation of God for the benefit of the world. And each writer creatively brings together several christological themes so that they interpret one another. But the various witnesses emphasize different aspects of the christological reality. No single text testifies for the whole of the church's Christology.

This variant christological emphasis is evident in the history of the church as well. The Chalcedonian formulation, for instance, seeks to interpret the event of Jesus Christ in categories of Hellenistic thought. Anselm and Abelard could agree with one another that the event of Jesus Christ is decisive, but each plots the nature of that decisiveness along a different axis.

Sample words and phrases illustrate the different ways the church has understood Jesus: bait for the devil, ransom, moral example, social reformer, liberator, feminist, unveiler of God's love, discloser of authentic existence, cosmocrator.

The preacher may find that a topical approach provides a very useful way to set forth the church's fundamental convictions concerning the event of Jesus Christ. The topical sermon allows the preacher to draw upon many resources of the past and present without being captive to any one of them. The sermon can be in recognizable continuity with Christian tradition even while performing its own function of interpreting the significance of Jesus Christ for its own moment.

When the text is only a springboard

Ministers sometimes use a biblical text only as a springboard to launch a topic. The preacher mentions a text in the sermon, but does not engage the text as a genuine "other," which has its own word to speak. The exposition of the text is not a controlling factor in the sermon. The text is little more than pretext.

Many of these occurrences are the result of genuine pastoral concern. The minister is aware of a need, issue, or situation, which is weighing on the heart of the congregation. The pastor deeply wants to help the congregation discover how the resources of the gospel can help lift the congregation's burden. The preacher begins sermon preparation with the text at hand, but something in the process of the study of the text sparks the preacher to orphan the text and to adopt the topic. Or, the preacher may simply make a free association between the text and the topic.

For instance, I once heard a minister begin a sermon with a sonorous reading of Isaiah 40:27–31. This passage climaxes in verse 31: "they who wait for the Lord shall renew their strength . . . they shall run and not be weary." The preacher went on, "Do you know what this means? It means that you should *run* your own life. You should take charge of your affairs." The sermon actually offered some useful hints for self-improvement (such as, you should be less passive and more assertive) but the sermon sounded as if it came out of a self-help book from the supermarket. The sermon was atextual and atheological and actually subverted the point of the pericope.

Some preachers come to the text with a fixed theological framework, which the text must fit. In the process of stretching the text to fit the framework, the text is bent unrecognizably out of shape. For instance, a sermon in early nineteenth-century Boston began with Joshua 10:22. Joshua has captured five Amorite kings in a cave and commands, "Open the mouth of the cave, and bring those five kings out to me from the cave." The preacher takes the five kings to be the five pillars of Calvinism: total depravity, unconditional election, limited atonement, irresistible grace, and the perseverance of the saints. The preacher then dismantles each of these pillars. The powerful narrative of the book of Joshua disappears.[6]

These examples may seem bizarre or dated. But, to be candid, each of us overlays a text with our own presuppositions, expectations, values, and theological innuendoes from time to time (if not more often). The use of a text as a springboard to get the sermon into the air is seldom the result of intentional manipulation or malevolence. It comes about because the preacher is not sufficiently self-conscious or critical.

Nonetheless, the practice is not in the best interests of the church. It misrepresents the preacher by leaving the impression that the preacher is dealing with the text. It misrepresents the text itself by leaving the impression that the text is about the subject of the sermon. The preacher's thoughts about the topic may be altogether valid and nurturing, but it is dishonest to pass them off as if they derive from the specific biblical text. Also, doing so violates the integrity of the text.

Further, the use of a text as a jumping-off point for a discussion of a topic that is unrelated to the text insulates the congregation from encountering the news, the challenges, the possibilities, and problems of the text itself. Indeed, this custom teaches the congregation that the Bible is little more than a jewelry box of textual baubles which can be pulled out and hung around the neck of the sermon for a little flashy decoration.

When the preacher becomes aware of using the text as a springboard into a topic, the preacher might do one of two things. First, the minister could postpone the discussion of the topic while searching for a text which has a genuine hermeneutical relationship with it. Or, secondly, the preacher could simply preach in the topical mode.

When hermeneutical movement is imprecise

An important chamber in the heart of expository preaching is the hermeneutical movement from the "then" of the text to the "now" of our world. But, at times, eagerly wanting to get from the biblical world to our world, we make hermeneutical movements that are imprecise. We follow the wrong hermeneutical map, so to speak. Sometimes, these moves are merely misleading. At other times they are harmful. Such miscalculations result not from the malfunction of the Bible itself but from the misjudgment of the preacher.

One pastor approached the subject of AIDS from Luke 5:27–32.[7] Levi, a tax collector, holds a feast in his home where large numbers of tax collectors and sinners eat with Jesus. The Pharisees and scribes murmur against Jesus. Jesus defends his ministry by saying, "Those who are well have no need of a physician, but those who are sick; I have not come to call the righteous, but sinners to repentance."

The message begins by recalling the importance of eating

together in the ancient world. By eating with tax collectors and sinners Jesus embodied God's care and acceptance for them. The Pharisees and scribes are outraged. However, according to the preacher, the smugness of the Pharisees is the real sickness in this text.

The minister then puts a question directly to us. "With whom are we refusing to sit? Through whom does Christ challenge us to perceive our own sickness? With whom does he call the Church to be 'more caring than careful?' "[8] With compassion, sensitivity, and insight, the pastor then calls the church to provide AIDS awareness information in the community and to mediate God's holy presence to AIDS victims.

This approach provides reliable guidance for Christians concerning possible roles for the church in AIDS ministries. But an aspect of the move from the text to the modern setting is imprecise and damaging. The message compares AIDS victims with tax collectors and sinners. In the world of Luke, tax collecting and sinning were explicitly immoral activities. As is well known, tax collectors were considered traitors and extortioners. Furthermore, E. P. Sanders has shown that many first-century Jews used the word *sinners* to refer to persons who overtly and willfully engaged in evil actions and who showed no inclination to repent.[9]

The minister does not dwell on the comparison between AIDS victims and the tax collectors and sinners. But the connection is implicit. To compare the church's ministry with AIDS patients with Jesus' ministry with the immoral is to imply that all AIDS victims are in the same ethical category as tax collectors and sinners.

Ryan White, a grade-school student from Kokomo, Indiana, contracted AIDS from a blood transfusion. Ryan White was not a Kokomo tax collector or a sinner. Neither are many AIDS sufferers today. Certainly, some AIDS victims do contract the disease by using contaminated needles for intravenous injections of illegal drugs or by sexual promiscuity. But, increasingly, the infection is spreading by means that are not willfully evil.[10]

The association of AIDS victims with tax collectors and sinners is unfortunate for many AIDS victims and their networks of family and friends. It misinterprets their situation and adds unnecessarily to their burdens. It also miseducates the congregation.

Again, preachers have two choices. If preachers want to engage AIDS issues in the pulpit, they could wait until they locate a text that offers a more precise hermeneutical relationship with the issue. Or they could preach a topical sermon that explores the disease, issues related to its transmission, dimensions of the Christian understanding of the illness itself, and the church's ministry to victims, to their families and friends, and to the larger culture.

When a text is harmful

I am reticent to give the harmful text a prominent place in the book because it is easily abused. A preacher may stumble upon what appears to be a difficulty in a text, and turn too quickly to this option without exploring the text and its hermeneutical possibilities in depth.

In some cases biblical texts articulate viewpoints that are not appropriate to the spirit of gospel, that are unintelligible, or (and) that may lead to immoral behavior. To present the questionable text as an authoritative word for the guidance of the church and the world is to do a disservice.

The preacher should proceed with caution when confronted by a text that appears to articulate dubious witness. Sandra M. Schneiders, speaking for a growing body of interpreters, points out that scripture is sometimes *used* ideologically to justify oppression, exploitation, and abuse even when the *content* of a text is not intrinsically inappropriate, unintelligible, or immoral.[11] Generations of human beings have ravaged the environment under the impression that we were commissioned to do so by the charge to humankind to subdue the earth in Genesis 1:28.[12] Recent scholarship now recognizes this interpretation of Genesis 1:28 as a mistake. When heard on its own terms, the text intends to encourage a relationship of mutuality between humankind and nature.[13] The trouble is not in the text itself but in the way the text has been heard. The preacher's responsibility in this case is to correct the way we understand the text.

But there are texts with troubles that cannot be explained away by misuse. "Here the problem is not that scripture has been used to legitimate oppression (although this is a continuing problem) but that the Bible itself is both a product and producer of oppression, that some of its *content* is oppressive."[14]

In a strange twist of events, the resurgence of biblical preaching in the last twenty years has exacerbated some problems in which the Bible is implicated. Texts that manifest anti-Judaism provide an illustration. Clark Williamson notices that in published sermons of the 1940s and 1950s, preachers tended to be less anti-Jewish than in published sermons of the 1970s and 1980s.[15]

In the middle of our century, before the biblical theology movement made a widespread impact on the pulpit, sermons often had a topical character. Many of these sermons do portray Christianity as superior to Judaism and many do downplay the value and even validity of Judaism. But the topical preachers of the previous generation do not talk as stridently (or as much in caricature) about the Jewish people of the first century as the preachers of the 1970s and 1980s.

Many of these latter-day preachers are committed to biblical preaching. Many texts from the gospels (and from other places as well) do contain anti-Jewish elements.[16] In the process of exposition, the preacher dwells on the negative qualities the text attributes to Jews and Judaism. In the worst scenarios, the Jewish community and Judaism itself "serve as images of everything bad in religion."[17] Such emphasis has the subtle effect of contributing not only to anti-Judaism but ultimately to anti-Semitism. This is especially ironic given that the 1970s and 1980s have been a period of growing dialogue and respect between Judaism and Christianity.

When faced with an intractable text, what does the preacher do? The minister might give an exposition of the meaning of the text and then show why the text is harmful and no longer authoritative.[18] (In the broad sense, I take this to be expository preaching.) Or the preacher might take a more topical approach. The appearance of a biting anti-Jewish text in the lectionary, for instance, might provide the pastor with a natural entree to helping the congregation reflect on the origins and history of anti-Judaism, on the Christian complicity therein, on how the gospel repudiates this phenomenon, and on practical things the congregation can do to work against anti-Judaism and anti-Semitism in our setting.

When there is no decisive Christian viewpoint

Occasionally, a need, issue, or situation emerges that invites comment but on which there seems to be no decisive Christian judgment. The dynamics and complexities of the topic are such that they cannot be simply and neatly put into boxes of "Christian" and "non-Christian." The minister senses the timeliness and propriety of speaking about the matter, but does not have a definitive word from the Lord.

For example, take the question of the economic system with which a community functions. Is one form of economy Christian to the exclusion of all others? Sincere Christians disagree about how to answer this question. Many prefer some form of democratic socialism. These Christians often indict capitalism, especially the United States version, with bloody, global exploitation, greed, and abuse. But socialist communities do not have an unblemished record of maintaining and improving the human community. Indeed, we now know that Marxists can be as exploitative, greedy, and abusive as the most rapacious board members of a transnational corporation. It *seems* to me that socialism has a better chance to maximize love and justice in the daily economic practices of a community. But as long as an economy is operated by finite creatures, I cannot say with unqualified certainty that socialism is *the* Christian way.

When faced with a topic on which there is no decisive Christian interpretation, the pastor may actually do the congregation a great favor by preaching on the topic. The sermon could delimit the topic, explore its issues and ambiguities, acknowledge the difficulties of coming to a definitive Christian conclusion, and assess the points at which the topic coincides with (and diverges from) the gospel. Ministers could indicate their preferences with regard to the topic, but indicate the provisional nature of such preferences.

This type of sermon might be a great relief to members of the community who sense the ambiguities of the topic but who had thought that, somehow, there must be *a* Christian interpretation of the topic which they had not understood. Such a sermon helps the congregation acknowledge the complexity of life. The sermon may encourage the congregation to take responsibility for its own judgments and preferences, even while acknowledging their relativity. And the sermon could enlarge the congregation's sense of humility: "We don't have all the answers."

A danger is that preacher and congregation will use the complexity of an issue as a cop-out. Instead of wrestling with an issue and risking a controversial or painful conclusion, the Christian community may too quickly wrap the issue in a blanket labeled, "No decisive Christian viewpoint." Some may sleep peacefully for a while. But like the infant who was put to bed before drinking a full bottle, they will cry again before the night is over.

Conclusion

One practical item remains before we go to the next chapter: the selection of a reading from the Bible for the service of worship when the topical sermon is preached. Some topical sermons do suggest scripture readings (for example, when the text is harmful). Other topical sermons make reference to passages from the Bible without dwelling on them (for example, when the topic is larger than a single text). In these instances, the worship planners could choose a text that is mentioned in the sermon and that represents the concern of the sermon. But some topical sermons pass by on the other side of the Bible. On such occasions the minister may select a pericope that relates in some way to the drift of the sermon or to its theological mooring.

In all cases, the integrity of the Bible is to be honored. Worship leaders do not want to leave the false impression that a reading sets the course for the sermon when it really does not. So, when the Bible reading is not integral to the sermon, the reader may accompany the text with a succinct comment that explains the relationship between the text and the sermon. This would both respect the text and help prepare the congregation for the sermon.[19]

CHAPTER THREE

PREPARING
THE TOPICAL SERMON

DISCIPLINED PREPARATION IS ONE OF THE KEYS TO RESPONSIBLE preaching.[1] Because of the ease with which the topical sermon can be abused, the pastor should be sure that the topical sermon is well grounded theologically and is not just a from-the-pulpit form of the latest trend in the social sciences.

To help with disciplined preparation, this chapter proposes eighteen steps of research, reflection, and imagination to lead to a topical sermon. Step 1 will help the preacher determine whether the topic is fitting for a whole sermon. Steps 2–10 will aid in identifying and interpreting fundamental issues in understanding the topic. Steps 11–13 move to a conclusion regarding how to understand the topic in the Christian house. Steps 14–18 assist in deciding upon a homiletical strategy that will have a good chance of drawing the listeners into conversation with the topic.

On a given topic, some steps will assume larger importance than others, while some other steps may all but disappear. This list may not be all-inclusive. Some may discover that I have overlooked an angle of vision that is critical for a particular sermon. While I have laid out these steps in linear fashion, a preacher may well find that they take place in inverted order or even simultaneously. In any event, preachers typically adapt models of sermon preparation to their own personalities, work habits, and ministerial settings.

A topical sermon usually has one of two foci: it may interpret a personal or social topic or it may explicate a matter of Christian doctrine. Of course, the preacher interprets personal and social topics through the window of systematic theology. Christian doctrine always has personal and social implications. (See Appendixes D and E respectively for works on preaching on social and personal issues and Christian doctrine.)

1. Determine that the topic is of sufficient size for the pulpit

By definition, the gospel is concerned with the whole of life. Therefore, the range of subjects possible for the topical sermon is limited only by life itself. But we need some boundaries so that the pulpit will not be taken over by trivia.

Buttrick posits three criteria to help determine whether a topic is of sufficient size and importance for the pulpit.[2] (a) The topic should connect with significant "ontological or historical questions." The topic has to do with what it means to be and to live. The topic brings into focus the ways in which we perceive God, ourselves, our world, our relationships, our values, and our actions.

(b) The topic should relate to "the store of unanswered questions which have been filed in consciousness by recurring limit moments or decision moments, crucial questions of meaning and morality." The topic deals with real-life matters in which something is at stake for the Christian community. These may be matters of understanding or of action.

(c) The topic "fits into the structures of Christian consciousness." The topic is one that the church can consider in the light of the gospel and its norms. In most instances the interpreta-

tion of the topic presents the listeners with a choice (of understanding or action), which can be made either appropriately or
inappropriately. But at times, the community cannot come to
a decisive normative judgment. In the latter case, the sermon
could perform the service of helping the community recognize
the ambiguities of the situation and those points at which the
Christian vision is instructive.[3]

These criteria cannot be applied mechanically to every
topic. Each topic presents itself in a particular historical moment which has its own distinctive characteristics. The forces
at work in a given time affect how we perceive the significance
of a topic. Therefore, a preacher's accuracy in reading the signs
of the times is crucial.

2. *Identify preassociations with the topic*

A preacher seldom brings a blank slate to the study of a topic.
A preacher nearly always has some preassociations with the
topic. These include feelings, memories, images, impressions,
questions, thoughts, judgments. They range from naive emotion to firm conclusion. The congregation will likely also have
preassociations.

Preassociations affect how the preacher and the congregation approach the topic. If the preassociations are left un-
identified and unexamined, they can predetermine the
community's encounter with the topic. As Walter Brueggemann notices, preassociations can operate as hidden, powerful vested interests, which orient the community (including
the preacher) to perceive the topic according to their own
biases.[4] In the worst instances, preassociations control the pastor's encounter with the topic to the extent that the sermon is
simply a canonization of them.

Recent hermeneutics has taught us that we are never completely neutral or value-free as we engage a text or a topic. Our
preassociations are inherently a part of our conversation.[5]

However, we should become conscious of these preassociations, so that we are not blindly manipulated by them (as by an ideology) and so that we can be critical of their role in our encounter with the topic. On the positive side, our preassociations can become resources for our encounter with the topic if we perceive them in critical perspective. And the preacher can often make use of them in the sermon.

The following exercises and questions may help flush preassociations to the surface of a pastor's awareness.

a. Let your mind associate freely with the topic. Record your free associations. Do you detect patterns in these associations, especially patterns that would affect your encounter with the topic?

b. What emotions stir in you as you consider the topic? How do these predispose you toward the topic?

c. What images focus on the screen of your mind as you consider the topic? What do these images reveal about your preorientation to the topic?

d. What questions spark in your mind as you meditate on the topic?

e. What would you say, right now, if you were asked, "Reverend, what is your opinion about this topic?" Are you willing to risk the possibility that sermon preparation might change this opinion, perhaps radically?

f. What are the points in the topic that you have difficulty understanding? Where does it rub you the wrong way?

g. Where do you sense gaps in your knowledge and understanding of the topic?

h. Do you really *care* about the topic? Suppose the journey of sermon preparation leads you to a conclusion that is painful or controversial. Do you think you would be willing to live with the aftermath of the sermon?

i. Which of these preassociations seems most "loaded,"

most capable of intruding inappropriately onto your interaction with the topic?

j. Can your preassociations serve as resources in your interaction with the topic or in the sermon?

At this point, nothing is evaluated. Nothing is too simple or too strange to be put on the table. The major purpose of this exercise is to locate preassociations that might lend an unrecognized hand in sermon preparation. But the exercise might also expose some material that could be directly helpful in the sermon. For instance, item *f* may bring out points at which you have difficulty with the topic. A point of difficulty is sometimes a place to begin the sermon.

For example, Susan, a Euro-American pastor, plans a sermon on relationships between Caucasians and people of color on the Sunday nearest the birthday of Martin Luther King, Jr. Susan's parents were respectable, middle-class, Republican laborers. She went to a small private college and a fine seminary. But her upbringing, education, and now ministry are located in a part of the country where there are very few African-Americans.

Susan works through these questions and discovers a layer of low-intensity prejudice. For example, her dominant image of the African-American woman is Aunt Jemima. She remembers feeling nervous while sharing a bus seat with an African-American the last time she was in Chicago. Although a new minister came to the tiny, struggling African Methodist Episcopal Zion Church on the far side of the town more than six months ago, Susan has not stopped to say "Welcome" and does not even know the name of her new colleague. She laughed at a joke at the ministerial association which used watermelon to make humor at the expense of African-Americans.

This pastor is intellectually committed to liberation. But without being really aware of it, Susan's energy for the sermon is diminished by low-intensity prejudice. Even if the sermon is theologically correct, these vestiges would likely drain the sermon of some of its passion and urgency. However, the pastor who becomes conscious of such preassociations can also become critical of them and may be able to draw upon them in the sermon itself.

3. List everything you need to know about the topic

A systematic plan by which to get into the world of the topic will often be a help to the minister. A systematic method of research increases the likelihood that a pastor will get the big picture of the topic and will see the focal points clearly. A large-screen view gives the pastor a sense of perspective on the tantalizing bits and pieces of information that nearly always result from careful research.

A simple way to organize one's approach to the topic is to make a list of everything that one needs to know about the topic in order to discuss it intelligently. Such a list will often help the preacher concentrate on the origin and history of the topic, on the current manifestation of the topic and issues relative to it, and on theological resources with which to understand and evaluate the topic from the viewpoint of the Christian community. (Items 4–11 in this chapter suggest areas for study that will frequently be useful.)

For many of us, research is synonymous with books and libraries. And to be sure, valuable information about a topic can often be found in one's pastoral library, in the local public library or bookstore, or in a nearby college library. The minister may also discover presentations on the topic in the media or the arts, on video or audio tape, in journals, or in conversation at a local coffee shop. In addition, a member of the congregation may be well acquainted with the topic. Seeking a member's aid will enhance the priesthood of all believers and bring into the sermon a source that is particularly credible to the listeners who know and trust the member.

For example, local comments lead the pastor to decide to help the congregation begin to reflect on the relationship between the gospel and various forms of government. Several war veterans indicate that democracy is God's only form of government. The pastor is tempted to preach a sermon that castigates the congregation for confusing democracy for theocracy. "God did not write the constitution of the United States." "The vote of the people cannot be confused with the will of God. Would God put [a certain corrupt elected official] into office?" "You have turned democracy into an idol." "God is not a member of the Republican Party." But after further thought, the pastor concludes that as presently conceived, the sermon would be a cheap shot. Likely it would anger local members to the point that they would not seriously reflect on the matter. Instead of bold prophecy, the sermon would mainly be a way for the preacher to express animosity toward the veterans. So, the pastor decides to take an approach that is more informed by history, theology, and critical analysis. The sermon will be passionate but will be less dictated by emotions.

The preacher begins a list of topics to be investigated. What are the origins and practices of democracy? What other forms and practices have organized human community (for example, theocracy, monarchy, tribal councils, dictatorship)? What forms of government appear in the Bible? How did the biblical communities understand these roles and how were they evaluated? How has the church viewed various types of government in its history? What factors contributed to the founders of the United States selecting democracy as the form of government for the new nation? Has the nation really functioned as a democracy? How has the denomination understood the relationship of church and state, of gospel and democracy? What do thoughtful Christians today think about the human government and the gospel, about democracy? What are the fundamental theological issues in the consideration of the topic? How does the sovereignty of God relate to the vote of the people? Is it possible for the gospel to be embodied in a democratic system? Do other systems have greater potential to embody the gospel? If several different patterns of social organization can embody the gospel, can the preacher identify "constants" which Christians regard as necessary in any and every pattern of government?

The credibility of the sermon is at stake. Almost certainly, the congregation contains members and friends who are knowledgeable about the topic. Their trust in the sermon is directly proportional to the preacher's accuracy in presenting information. This is especially true of controversial issues when the preacher's conclusion runs against the grain of the congregation's mindset. The careful preacher will research viewpoints and conclusions on all sides of the issue so as to represent them fairly.

4. Search for biblical perspectives

The Bible sometimes contains perspectives that illumine the topic. The best way to get into the Bible is to engage it directly. When that is not possible, a thorough concordance is a good companion to lead the minister into the world of the Bible.[6] An up-to-date Bible dictionary provides a convenient summary of major biblical positions and passages (as well as major interpretive discussions). (For helps in biblical interpretation, see Appendix F.) However, ministers need to be careful not to let the Bible dictionary or other resource stand between them and the Bible itself.

When preparing a sermon on the doctrine of the Holy Spirit, for example, the preacher would try to discern the nature of the Spirit, its modes of activity, and significant passages. One might discover that the Spirit is predominantly an agent of God. The Spirit can be manifest as an agent of creation, or as mediating the knowledge of the presence of God, or as a life-force which sustains the world, or as special empowerment for ecstasy or insight which leads to particular tasks (such as leadership in battle or prophecy), or as a tie which regathers the scattered members of the human family, or as a sign and promise of the eschaton. A few focal passages include Genesis 1:1–2; Job 34:14–15; Psalm 139:7–12; Isaiah 42:1–4; 61:1–4; Joel 2:28–32; Matthew 1:18–26; 3:13–17; 28:16–20; Luke 4:14–30; John 14:15–26; 20:19–23; Acts 2:1–21; Romans 8:1–30; 1 Corinthians 12–14; Galatians 5:16–26.

A careful researcher recognizes that different biblical writers emphasize different aspects of the Spirit's work. Likely, the preacher will turn up more material than can be used in a single sermon and will have to be quite selective regarding what can be used in the message itself.

Three circumstances may call for particular comment in the sermon: (a) When the Bible is silent on the topic. This awareness may be genuinely informative for the congregation. When the preacher mentions in the sermon the silence of the Bible, the community should recognize that the preacher has sought the guidance of scripture and will not suspect the preacher of ignoring the Bible.

(b) When the Bible contains more than one viewpoint on the topic. On some issues the Bible speaks with many different voices (as on the Holy Spirit). When the preacher brings this diversity to the attention of the hearers, they are reminded that we cannot simply mechanically reproduce the Bible's viewpoints in our own time. We must think for ourselves and use the biblical witnesses as instructive conversation partners.

(c) When the Bible is harmful. In those rare instances when the Bible takes a stand that is inappropriate to the gospel, unintelligible, or morally implausible, the preacher can help the congregation identify the difficulty and recognize that the text does not have the congregation in a hammerlock. The gospel itself is a higher authority in the church than the text.[7]

5. Trace how the topic has been interpreted in the history of the church

With the exception of religious professionals, today's Christian community is not well acquainted with the life and thought of the church from the mid-second century C.E. to the present. The preacher renders an important service to the Christian body by bringing appropriate voices from the post-canonical past into the sermon. At the general level, doing so helps the church of today overcome its historical amnesia. At the specific level, the post-biblical tradition may contain voices which contribute directly to our understanding of the topic. For instance, several figures from the past speak with force on the question of whether it is permissible for a Christian to serve in the military. Their thoughts can be quite provocative (on all sides of the issue) as we consider conscientious objection. Sometimes the material is indirect or analogous. Not surprisingly, no one in the church, prior to the last quarter of the twentieth century, commented on the potential merger of the Christian Church (Disciples of Christ) and the United Church of Christ. Yet, members of these denominations can be richly instructed by paying attention to ways in which previous councils and leaders thought through matters of ecumenical relationship. Sometimes, of course, the tradition is silent.

It may sound overwhelming to think of tracing how the church has understood a topic from the mid-second century C.E. to the present. But two factors help pare the assignment down to manageable size. One, the voices that speak on a given topic usually cluster around a few significant viewpoints. The second is that many topics are discussed in survey articles in dictionaries and encyclopedias of Christian thought. (See Appendix G for theological reference works.) Such articles give the preacher a macroview of the topic and point to specific figures and resources for detailed study. Further, research on the topic often turns up a book or journal article which succinctly overviews the history of the topic.

Such surveys can be liberating. For example, the stewardship drive comes around every year. Some pastors weary of talking about money, and fear that they are actually shrinking their congregations' notions of stewardship to that of writing checks to the church. It may come as a source of new stewardship energy to discover that the limited idea of stewardship as voluntarily contributing to the church budget is a relatively recent (and somewhat North American) phenomenon.[8] As a biblical concept, stewardship refers to the response of our whole lives to the grace of God. Thus, Douglas John Hall, one of the leading authorities on stewardship in our time, writes not of how to sell the church budget to skeptical parishioners but of "the stewardship of life in the kingdom of death."[9]

6. Focus on two theologians on the topic

The previous step gives the preacher a macroview, which shows the broad outlines of the topic. By focusing on what two theologians have to say about the topic, the preacher gains two microviews. The contrast is similar to the differences between a landscape painting of the Rocky Mountains and a character study of an aged Native American woman's face.

Much of the time, it will benefit the minister if one of the theologians comes from the past and the other from the present. The earlier representative's thought can help us in two ways. We commonly say that it is easier to see mistakes (and to note proportions of strength) in retrospect than in the midst of a situation. Such assessment is frequently true of theological argument as well. By turning to a theologian of the past, we can see where this thinker pierced to the heart of a topic and where accuracy of information, logic, or perspective failed.

A contemporary theologian is often sensitive to the cultural dynamics in which current congregations find themselves. Contemporaries often speak in language that is immediately accessible to current listeners. Indeed, today's theologians often open windows on our situation which we have not thought to open and which allow us to have a better under-standing of why things happen around us as they do. Further, a theologian provides a contemporary viewpoint that a pastor can use as a "test case." Where are the points of strength? Where are the points that do not withstand scrutiny? What do I, as a leader in the church, learn from this theologian's content and method that helps me as I move toward formulating my own judgments on the topic? Does the theologian see subtle-ties (or large trends) that I have missed?

This part of the preparation of the topical sermon will prob-ably come as second nature to pastors. Most of us identify with a theological tradition (such as fundamentalist, evangelical, liberal, neoorthodox, process, or liberation) and with specific figures within the tradition. A danger of such familiarity is that a minister can become anesthetized to other viewpoints. Min-isters can often help keep their theological passageways open by self-administering the smelling salts of other theological viewpoints. A Barthian who has labored in isolated rural com-munities for thirty years might become radically awake by reading I. Carter Heyward's feminist, liberation, lesbian the-ology.[10]

7. Bring out the denomination's position on the topic

When preaching in a setting which is related to a denomina-tion, a responsible pastor will consult the denomination's po-sition(s) on the topic. Pastors may find that awareness of the denomination's position helps them clarify their own perceptions. In the best case, the denomination's statement may help the pastor grow. It may even be a fulcrum that the preacher can set so as to get the best leverage as the sermon attempts to push against the congregation. In the worst case, the discovery of the denomination's conclusion may leave the preacher livid.

Obtaining the denomination's statements is relatively easy in groups that publish comprehensive, official compendia, which bring together the church's wisdom on doctrine and on needs, issues, and situations that face the church. The United Methodist Church, for example, publishes *The Book of Discipline*.[11] At the other end of the spectrum, my own denomination, the Christian Church (Disciples of Christ), does not have a highly evolved central nervous system. We simply pass resolutions from one international meeting to the next, without bringing the resolutions into systematic coherence with one another and without even compiling a directory of the denomination's common beliefs, policies, and resolutions.

When the denomination's upper judicatory has not published its own position on a topic, the preacher may find that a denominational task force or a denominational thinker has brought out a report on the topic which helps the minister get a sense of the denomination's concerns. For example, the general synod may not have taken a vote on English as the official language for publication of government documents and for instruction in the public schools. But a church located in an area with a large Hispanic population may have appointed a task force that produced a report and recommendation on this very issue.

A judicious pastor will be clear about the nature and authority of churchly statements. Some denominational bodies speak authoritatively and unambiguously for the whole church. Other bodies speak only for themselves. A general assembly may speak only for the few thousand members who actually attend the assembly. The honesty of the sermon requires alerting the congregation to such discriminations.

A sensitive preacher will also try to respect multiple positions on a topic. In the first part of this century, for instance, the United Methodist Church and its predecessor bodies were noted for disapproval of the use of alcohol, but many Methodists used alcohol anyway. In recent years, this emphasis has diminished. However, in some congregations the use of liquor is still unofficially disapproved. This history affects the listening climate in many United Methodist congregations when the pastor begins a sermon on alcoholism or on the morality of holding stock in corporations that manufacture alcoholic beverages. A preacher who plays fast and loose with the denomination's often complicated, and highly emotional, history will alienate many listeners before the listeners have a chance to consider the issues in a fair way.

8. Investigate other relevant dimensions of the topic

Our knowledge of a topic is often enriched by disciplines and perspectives that range beyond conventional religious sources. Enriching contributions come from such sources as history, psychology, sociology, political science, ecology, economics, the arts, and the natural sciences. As already noted in this chapter, the informed use of such data can be crucial for maintaining the respect and credibility of the listener. Moreover, the integrity of the sermon itself requires that a preacher have a full and accurate grasp of the topic.

When developing a sermon on domestic violence, for instance, the preacher wants to know what we mean by domestic violence, who and how many are affected, where it takes place and under what circumstances, and what it does to the victims. The preacher looks into the psychological factors that operate in the person who commits acts of violence. The preacher is also interested in cultural and systemic factors that contribute to domestic conflict. The preacher is curious about the steps that are necessary to intervene in patterns of domestic violence, about structures that help people escape from violent situations and that help violent offenders recognize and deal with their tendencies.

One must beware lest these materials take over the sermon. We are schooled to respect empirical data. On a given topic, empirical analysis may be plenteous and impressive. The preacher can easily be beguiled into reading several pages from a sociologist's printed work and calling it a sermon. So, while such data is essential, the preacher makes the best use of it by reflecting on what it reveals about the news of God's unconditional love for all as well as God's will for justice for all.

9. Inventory the congregation's experience with the topic

Step 2 recommends a process for becoming cognizant of the pastor's preassociation with the topic. The present step calls for a systematic determination of the congregation's experience with the topic.[12]

Many of the sources for a congregational inventory are as close as the members of the congregation. An important pastoral preparation for the congregational inventory is to let the topic become like an extra set of glasses through which the pastor views the congregation or like a hearing aid through which the pastor listens to the congregation. When these are tuned to the topic, any encounter with the congregation may bring in material that adds to the inventory. A written congregational history might contain information pertinent to the topic's history in a local community. And, of course, general resources of cultural awareness (for example, the coffee shop, the newspaper, the electronic media, short stories, and novels) play an informative role.

The following are some leading questions that can help fill out a picture of the congregation's experience with the topic.

a. What are the congregation's memories and preassociations with the topic? (The pastor may find it useful here to ask questions from step 2 about the congregation.)
b. How do these memories tend to orient the congregation positively or negatively toward the topic?
c. Where, and how, does the congregation come into contact with the topic today?
d. What are the major incidents that seem to contribute to the congregation's experience with the topic?
e. What are the congregation's feelings about the topic? How deep are these feelings and how aware of them is the congregation?
f. What are the congregation's convictions regarding the topic? Are these convictions the result of serious thinking about the topic or are they naive (though deeply held)?
g. What are the congregation's fears and hopes around the topic?
h. What does the congregation see as the future of the topic?

A congregation contains many members, and the members may not share the same experience of the topic. In fact, a congregation may be a microcosm of the diversity of experience which is found in the larger culture. But even diverse bodies often have a center of gravity where a significant body of the congregation's experience can be taken into account.

Suppose a preacher is developing a topical sermon on the Christian understanding of sin. Through pastoral listening, the minister works up an inventory on the congregation's experience and understanding of sin. The pastor discovers that many of the congregation's earliest memories of sin are associated with naughty deeds. Many in the congregation went through a Sunday school class in which the teacher used the image of a worm to get the students to see what it means to be a sinner.

As adults, many think of sin in association with sexuality. Playing charades at a class party, one couple is asked to pantomime the hymn "Rock of Ages." When they come to the line "Be of sin, the double cure," the couple covers their sexual organs (suggesting that sex is a sin that needs a double cure).

Some members may echo classical formulations of sin (such as an enslaving power; as alienation from God, neighbor, and self; failure to trust God; or distortion of relationship). But on the whole, the congregation's perception of the topic will likely be limited to sin as individual moral actions. The preacher thus discovers that consciousness-raising needs to be an important aspect of the sermon.

10. Imagine what it is like to be different persons in different situations relative to the topic

The minister (and the congregation) can enlarge their perception of the topic by imagining what it is like to be different persons in different situations relative to the topic.[13] This exercise can help the preacher and the listener develop empathy with the topic itself and with the different ways in which the topic affects people.

The most obvious application of this exercise is in respect to those who are directly affected by the topic. For instance, in the case of a topical sermon on alcoholism, the preacher can imagine what it is like to be an alcoholic, to be married (or formerly married) to an alcoholic, to be the child (including an adult child) of an alcoholic, to be a friend, or an employer, or a parent of an alcoholic.

The approach can also be used to good effect in the case of those who will hear the sermon. What is it like, for instance, to be a listener who will hear a sermon on alcoholism? How will the sermon sound to an alcoholic? How will it fall on the ears of a spouse of an alcoholic? A parent? A friend? An employer? How will the topic seem to someone who, to this point, has been able to drink alcohol without noticeable degenerative effects? And how will the members of the Women's Christian Temperance Union react?

This exercise can be useful with almost any topic, but it can be especially valuable when dealing with controversial topics. If the preacher can imagine what it is like to be a listener who is afraid of the topic, or hostile to the topic, the preacher may be able to design a homiletical approach which will not immediately push the detonator on the explosive mind of the listener but will give the listener an opportunity to consider the topic on its own terms.

11. Evaluate the topic theologically

The theological evaluation of the topic is the heart of preparing the topical sermon. In order to facilitate this process, I draw upon three criteria that can be applied to any subject or situation.[14]

(a) Appropriateness to the gospel. Is the phenomenon of the topic, and the ways in which people understand it and respond to it, appropriate to the gospel? Does the topic manifest God's unconditional love for each and all as well as God's will for justice for each and all?

(b) Intelligibility. This is a criterion of the degree to which the topic (and our understanding of it and response to it) makes sense. The norm operates on two levels. On the first level, the standard of intelligibility has to do with the internal logic of the Christian faith. Does the topic (and our grasp of it) make sense in the light of what we otherwise believe in the Christian house? On the second level, the criterion helps us relate our late-twentieth-century worldview to the topic. We evaluate the topic against the norms of what we normally believe to be true about the world and its operation. We also question what we think about the world in the light of the topic. Does the topic (and our human perspectives on it) make sense in the light of what we otherwise think to be true of the world? Admittedly, this is the most enigmatic of the norms of judgment.

(c) Moral plausibility. The third norm focuses on the moral treatment of all who are related to the topic, including the inarticulate world of nature. Moral treatment is that which asserts God's love for all in every situation and which works toward justice for all in every situation.

These three criteria are not completely distinct. They overlap, but each has its own accent.

In the summer of 1990, Iraq invaded Kuwait. The United States took a leading role in getting the United Nations Security Council to pass resolutions demanding that Iraq vacate Kuwait. The resolutions authorized economic sanctions against Iraq in the hope that they would cause Iraq to withdraw. If Iraq did not return Kuwait by January 15, 1991, the resolutions authorized a coalition of nations (headed by the United States) to take military action to force Iraq to withdraw. Iraq did not adhere to the resolutions. The coalition initiated war with Iraq.

The war had a high degree of popular support in the United States, but many in the Christian community questioned how Christians should understand this war (and other wars). United States spokespeople used the "just-war" theory to support military action against Iraq. This theory, the roots of which are as old as Augustine, holds that a war is "just" if it is not a war of aggression, if its cause is right, if it is declared by legitimate authorities, if it is fought so as to minimize killing and damage, and if the war is a last resort to rectify an injustice.

Was the war against Iraq appropriate to the gospel? Killing never demonstrates unconditional love for other persons.

Was the war intelligible? Advocates of the just-war theory attempted to show that the war was just. For instance, the actions of war were to be proportional to the goal of securing the release of Kuwait from Iraqi occupation. The military actions taken against Iraq were designed to destroy only military installations, equipment, and personnel, and to minimize damage to civilians. Even so, the war still resulted in the death of many Iraqis and in the destruction of resources and services that support life. In this respect, war can never be *just* in the full Christian sense of the term. Indeed, the idea of a "just war" is an oxymoron in Christian logic. A community may conclude that monstrous evil can be controlled only by means of violence, but such a conclusion is cause for weeping and penitence and never for flag-waving and brass bands.

Many were convinced that the United States did not allow the sanctions sufficient time to have an effect. To be sure, sanctions are more humane than Stealth bombers and Tomahawk missiles, but sanctions still damage the quality of life for others. The behavior of the nation-states in this conflict points to the need to reread (to use Buttrick's language[15]) the very notion of the nation-state as the principal means by which the peoples of the world organize themselves into human communities and relate to one another. It also points out the need to establish worldwide love and justice. As long as nations exploit other nations to gain creature comforts, it is only a matter of time until another Iraq invades another Kuwait.

In the case of a doctrinal sermon, the preacher may not so much evaluate the doctrine as draw out how the doctrine helps us grasp the gospel in relationship to the doctrine. For instance, the doctrine of sanctification points us to the need (and the source of power) for us to continue growing in our love for God and for one another as well as in actions and attitudes that are just. However, doctrines, too, can be evaluated. How does the gospel square with the idea that God passes judgment upon a community through the destruction of that community?

12. State your own position on the topic

A brief, written paragraph helps the preacher develop a sharply defined position. Putting the summary of the position into writing pushes the preacher toward precision. When an idea hangs suspended in the mind, it can be tossed about by every passing wind. Writing helps the pastor give the idea a definite form. The written statement also gives the preacher a definite center point for ease in thinking critically about the position.

For instance, a preacher may think generally about giving a topical sermon on faith. "Ya gotta believe!" But what does the preacher mean by faith? Who is the principal actor in the faith relationship? How does one attain faith? What does faith mean to believers in specific circumstances? What are the implications of faith in one's politics or ecological practice? Writing will nudge the preacher away from the glittering generality of "Ya gotta believe" toward the specificity of the latter concerns.

At Christian Theological Seminary, students are assigned a topical sermon on faith. Semester after semester, similar reports emerge. "In the process of writing a statement on my position on the topic, I discovered that I was speaking of faith as a human achievement. I was making faith a work of justification. I was reducing the formula from justification by grace through faith to simply justification by faith. The sermon was well on its way to placing faith in the ledgerbook of works righteousness instead of offering it as a gift from our God through which we trust in God's grace as the basis for our self-understanding." The written statement typically allows the student to catch this particular warp before it twists the minds of the listeners.

13. Articulate viewpoints other than your own

It is also good to distill (in writing) the viewpoints of others. This regimen has six values. First, the simple act of putting other views down on paper encourages pastors to clarify their own perceptions.

Second, setting the judgments of others on paper physically reminds the preacher of the existence (and force) of other lines of interpretation.

Third, by entering different points of view on a piece of paper (or into a computer) a minister may be less likely to treat them in caricature and more likely to treat them fairly. When I have to *look* at another person in the flesh, I tend to be somewhat more objective about that person than when I am only thinking (or gossiping) about the person. A similar objectivity comes into play when I write down the viewpoints of others.

Fourth, considering the viewpoints of others helps the preacher understand why the others hold their viewpoints. It helps the preacher see why their viewpoints are important to them.

Fifth, as in step 12, the written form makes critical evaluation easier. The minister has a crisp and accurate portrait of the strengths and weaknesses of the others.

Sixth, the material may prove directly useful in the sermon itself. When the topic is controversial, the sermon becomes more credible to the listeners when the preacher openly and accurately acknowledges viewpoints other than the position being recommended in the sermon and when the preacher represents those viewpoints evenhandedly.

Suppose a community is voting on whether or not to institute a lottery. Members of the congregation become curious about the church's position on the lottery. Some in the congregation are playing old tapes in their heads that warn against gambling of any kind. Some oppose the lottery on the basis of hard, cold reasons. Others in the congregation glibly endorse the lottery: "Think of the taxes we won't have to pay!"

The minister feels uneasy when one family in the last group announces that they will donate ten percent of their winnings to the church's endowment fund. ("Should we accept that money or not?")

The pastor determines that the sermon will oppose the lottery because the lottery is not in the best interest of the public good. The preacher's research has discovered that lotteries tend to take money out of the pockets of those who can least afford it and actually to lower their quality of life. Lotteries inflame gambling addiction in many people, thus upsetting their households and communities. Lotteries create opportunities for corruption and organized crime. Lotteries encourage the idea of getting something for nothing and thereby have the subtle effect of discouraging the work ethic. Lotteries are unreliable sources of income for public life and works. The lottery thus works against God's call for universal justice.

However, the preacher also lists the reasons others in the congregation favor the lottery. Some of these ideas will appear in the sermon when the preacher acknowledges the "opposition case." The lottery does generate income for the local government without raising taxes. The community can have some things it would otherwise not have at the current tax rate (for example, computers in the local grade school). The winners will contribute to the economy by spending some of their winnings locally. Proponents argue that some people will gamble under any circumstances; the lottery enables the government to regulate this gambling and to profit from it. Further, people should be able to do what they want with their money. "This is a free country. This is what the U.S.A. is all about!"

Making the list helps the pastor be able to respond sympathetically but clearly to those who favor the lottery. The listeners who advocate the lottery have the satisfaction of knowing that the preacher has taken their position seriously. In a situation where there are winners and losers, the post-decision relationship between the two has a good chance of surviving in good health if the competition has been marked by a sense of fair play.

14. Consider the mindset and situation of the listeners in relationship to the topic

The process of sermon preparation takes account of the situation, mindset, and heartset of the listeners. Their orientation and receptivity to the topic can help the preacher settle upon a homiletical strategy that attempts to let the flow of congregational consciousness work with the sermon. An experienced canoeist knows how to ride the white water so that the turbulence does not endanger the craft so much as it speeds the canoe on its voyage and increases the maneuverability of the canoe. Much the same thing can happen in preaching; the sermon can be shaped and steered so that it takes advantage of the currents in the congregation. Steps 14 and 15 are intended to help the preacher chart the river of congregational consciousness and prepare the boat of the sermon. Seven questions can help bring the congregation's situation, mindset, and heartset into easy view.

    a. How do the listeners currently encounter the topic (steps 8–10)?

    b. What are their current predispositions and convictions concerning the topic (steps 8–10)?

    c. Is the congregation rightly informed about the topic?

    d. Are the congregation's perceptions about the topic appropriate to the gospel (step 11)?

    e. Are the congregation's perceptions and convictions intelligible (step 11)?

f. Are the congregation's perceptions, convictions, and behaviors (relative to the topic) morally plausible (step 11)?
g. What does the congregation most need relative to the topic: reinforcement? information? correction? challenge?

The answers to these questions can reveal important tasks for the sermon. For instance, if the congregation is misinformed at crucial points, the sermon needs to provide correct information. If the congregation holds convictions that are inappropriate to the gospel, the sermon needs to suggest how the congregation's convictions can be reshaped. If the congregation's views are deeply held but are outside the embrace of the Christian vision, the sermon will need to offer the Christian vision as an alternative that is more attractive and compelling than the one currently in place.

For example, after a long and difficult search, the congregation has bought new hymnals. They will be in the pews for the first time next Sunday and the minister will focus the sermon on introducing the new hymnal to the congregation. The process of selecting the new hymnal and preparing the sermon itself has given the preacher important clues to the congregation's mindset and heartset in relation to the new hymnal.

Although very few members have looked carefully through the new hymnal, there is a high degree of resistance to it. Several members have heard about changes in hymns for reasons of inclusivity; they do not understand this phenomenon and fear that it means the church is abandoning the historic Christian faith. Recently, the local newspaper ran an article from a national wire service under the headline "National Hymnal Committee Throws Out Great Old Hymns," including some local favorites. Some members on vacation worshiped at an avant-garde congregation where the hymnal is in use and reported that new, unfamiliar hymns crowd the pages: "Many of those songs do not even sound like church music."

The topic of the new hymnal is thus a sour note for many

in the congregation. The rumors and innuendoes that have been whispered through the congregation move the people into the realm of the morally implausible. The sermon is not the only vehicle to address this situation, of course, but the sermon can attempt to correct some of the misinformation (for example, the hymnal does contain a lot of hymns known and loved in the congregation). The sermon can also articulate a vision of how the hymnal can help the congregation enlarge its awareness of the gospel and its power to witness to the gospel.

15. Locate the listeners in relationship to your position on the topic

Step 14 gives the preacher a wide-angle view of the listeners' relationship to the *topic*. Step 15 is a close-up focus on the listeners' mindset and heartset with respect to the *position* the minister will advocate in the sermon.

If the congregation basically agrees with the minister, she or he may presume the good will of the congregation toward the topic. The sermon may go directly to the heart of the minister's concern. The mood of the sermon may be characterized as "Let's build on what we already have in common." In the optimum listening environment, the congregation greets the topic with joy and enthusiasm. The preacher's role is to harness and focus congregational energy.

For instance, the congregation has become excited about the possibility of building a senior citizens' housing complex on a big lot next to the church. The sermon can celebrate God's presence in mature adults and envision possibilities for enhancing the lives of mature adults (and, indeed, of the whole congregation) through the ministry of the complex.

In instances when the congregation disagrees with the minister's position, members of the congregation may have built hardened emotional and intellectual bunkers to defend against the very thesis of the sermon. Thus, the minister must think carefully about how to introduce the topic and his or her perspective so as to try to win the interest and trust of the listeners and to generate as little unnecessary interference as possible. Inductive approaches often help the sermon penetrate these bunkers.

For instance, the denomination's upper-level judicatory has passed a resolution asking church members to boycott the products of a transnational corporation because the corporation exploits third world workers and customers. Many of the congregations' influential members own stock in the transnational corporation. The preacher concludes that God's will for justice calls for a sermon in support of the denomination's resolution. But the preacher also knows that the congregation is actively hostile toward that position. So, the minister decides to build the sermon around a poignant story about a third world family whose life is interrupted by the use of the product. The preacher hopes that the congregation will empathize with the family and will join the preacher in the later stages of the sermon in asking, "What can we do to help this family and others like it?"

The congregation may not know where they stand in relationship to the preacher's position. They may be uninformed, in which case a primary responsibility of the sermon is to provide information in a captivating way. The congregation may not have a clear idea of how to separate the issues for consideration. In this case, the sermon is a knife in the hands of a skilled cook, cutting the topic into serving-size issues and showing where the preacher's position is joined to the carcass.

16. State what you want to say in the sermon

One of the axioms of homiletics is that the preacher write a single sentence which summarizes the thrust of the sermon.

This statement is usually drawn from the themes set down in step 12. I refer to this statement as the sermon-in-a-sentence.[16]

The sermon-in-a-sentence helps guide the preacher in developing thematic unity in the sermon. Everything in the sermon leads to, flows from, develops, illumines, enlarges, or otherwise relates to the sermon-in-a-sentence.

The most helpful sermon-in-a-sentence tends to be a simple sentence composed of subject, verb, and predicate. When the sermon-in-a-sentence becomes more complex, it is difficult to keep the sermon wound around a single spool of thought.

A sermon is fundamentally good news from God concerning God's love for the world and God's will for justice in the world.[17] This conviction has implications for the sermon-in-a-sentence: (a) The subject is normally God. (b) The verb is usually an activity of God. (c) The predicate is normally a benefit or other outflow of God's love and justice (as indicated in the verb). (d) The sermon-in-a-sentence is usually positive and offers the community hope and encouragement. Even when the community falls under indictment, the sermon-in-a-sentence seeks to show how the gospel empowers the congregation to move beyond its limitations.

For example, a congregation has a large population of single adults. Conventional church literature and programming has focused upon families (mom, dad, two children, a station wagon, and a shaggy dog). Some single people feel excluded. The pastor becomes aware of uneasiness in the congregation regarding the validity of the single life. The preacher decides that one way to address this uneasiness is through a sermon. The preacher develops the following sermon-in-a-sentence.

> God unconditionally loves single people and wills for single people to be fully accepted in the church as single people.

In the sermon, the pastor will articulate the uneasiness of the congregation regarding the single life. The minister may help the congregation pass judgment on some of its own attitudes and practices. The sermon will explore ways in which single persons can be integrated into the community. Ultimately, the preacher wants the sermon to embody the sermon-in-a-sentence so that the life of the congregation will be strengthened.

Normally, the sermon-in-a-sentence should not exhort the congregation to take action. In traditional theological language, the sermon majors in the indicative and minors in the imperative. The gospel is fundamentally good news. The preacher's preeminent task is to clarify the relationship of this news to the topic.

When the sermon has an indicative quality, it helps correct one of the most damaging problems of the church in our time: moralism.[18] When religion is reduced to moralism, *the* goal of the religious life is proper moral behavior. On the right end of the theological spectrum, moralism dwells on individual behavior (such as limiting promiscuous sexual activity) while on the left end of the spectrum it focuses on proper social behavior (such as supporting the proper political parties in Central America). It is a short step from moralism to works-righteousness.

Of course, there are times when the sermon legitimately calls the congregation to action. But the congregation's power to say "Yes" to these imperatives comes from the regular experience of the indicative.

17. Decide what you hope will be the result of the listener's hearing of the sermon

Of course, ministers hope that listeners will "get the point" of the sermon as stated in the preceding step. Sermon preparation has an additional sense of direction when preachers specify what they hope will happen in the congregation as a result of hearing the sermon. For convenience of presentation, we will speak of sermons that are generally oriented to the mind (understanding), oriented to the heart (feeling), and oriented to the will (action). Of course, the human being is a whole in which mind, heart, and will intertwine. Human experience cannot be divided into these neat categories. A powerful idea can unleash deep passions. I sometimes must make an act of the will (a decision) about whether to accept or reject a certain idea.

The preacher may hope that a given sermon leads the congregation to *understand* a topic in the terms of the gospel. The main goal of the sermon is for the listeners to become conscious of how the topic appears from the perspective of the Christian vision. For example, in a situation in which the congregation is confused about whether God's power is coercive or persuasive, a minister's guiding objective in a sermon might be to help the congregation understand the differences between these two ways of conceiving of God's power and why one of them is superior. When understanding is the goal of the sermon, the sermon can easily bog down in a morass of facts that are presented as dull and lifeless. Thus, the preacher needs to make a special effort to see that the sermon is interesting and life-related.

The preacher may hope that a given sermon helps the congregation *feel* some aspect of the topic. The sermon may be designed to lead the congregation into an imaginative experience of the topic. Through the language and imagery of the sermon, the minister may hope to touch the deep chords of the heart. For instance, a sermon concentrating on how the gospel participates in delivering people from depression could help the hearers identify their feelings of depression and could then create the sense of moving out of depression and into a full and free embrace of life.

A sermon with emphasis that falls upon the heart is not a sermon that is devoid of intellectual content. An emotive experience is most meaningful when it takes place within an interpretive framework that names the significance of the experience. Indeed, a major task of preaching in our time is to help the congregation claim (or reclaim) a Christian understanding of life and to charge that understanding with emotive power.

The preacher may hope that a given sermon leads a congregation to a willful *decision*, and perhaps even to an action. A sermon on God's persuasive power, for instance, may ask the listeners to decide whether they will understand God's power in that way and whether they will exercise power persuasively themselves.

18. Design the sermon so that it will have a good chance of accomplishing its purposes

The preacher now decides *how* to say *what* to say. The preacher wants the sermon to receive a fair (and positive) hearing by the community. This is a point of great pastoral creativity. Scholarly authorities in Cambridge, Chicago, Decatur, Dallas, and Claremont may have great insight into the topic, but they do not know the minds, hearts, and language of the listeners in the way that the pastor does.

Our discussion of deductive and inductive patterns of sermonic movement (in chapter 1) comes into play here. Will the sermon be inductive, deductive, or hybrid?

Long ago, Harold Bosley suggested that a preacher could take one of two routes into the topic: direct or indirect.[19] In the direct sermon, the preacher moves in a friendly way directly to the topic itself. This approach is amenable to topics that are not particularly controversial. In the indirect sermon, the preacher does not raise the topic directly, but moves obliquely from something familiar to and shared with the congregation to the topic itself. The indirect approach is thus particularly suitable for controversial topics.

Of course, there are many different indirect approaches to topical sermons. In one that is particularly promising, the preacher begins the sermon by laying the theological foundation for the discussion of the topic, but does so without reference to the topic itself. The preacher moves to the topic itself only in the later stages of the sermon.

This movement has three advantages, particularly when preaching on a controversial subject. First, as a communication strategy, it should raise a minimum of suspicions or defensiveness on the part of the congregation. Second, as more than a communication strategy, it embodies the priority and givenness of the gospel in the consideration of any situation. The gospel is not just an elixir for dealing with problems but is the life-force within which to understand existence and its problems. Third, this approach may help the listeners see that they are dealing not just with the preacher and the preacher's opinion on the topic; they are dealing with the Christian tradition itself.

A sermon might begin with the doctrine of justification by grace. We are already put in right relationship with God through no merit of our own. We do not, for instance, have to feed the hungry in order to be accepted by God. But when we accept justification by grace as the basis of our self-understanding, then we are obliged (by virtue of our identity as justified) to relate to others in ways that assert that we understand them to be already justified as well. Thus, we are compelled to feed the hungry.

Craddock's proposal for preaching that allows the listener to overhear the gospel should be mentioned here. Craddock observes that in many situations, our most penetrating experiences come as a result of overhearing others, in contrast to being addressed eyeball to eyeball on the subject.[20] A child lies in bed at night and, through the grate in the floor, overhears the parents in the kitchen below speaking of their love and tenderness for the child. The child drifts to sleep with the conversation in the kitchen washing the wounds from the spat after supper and wrapping the child in security which could not come in the still emotionally charged moment when the parent had said, "Look, let's just forget about this incident and start over."

Topical preachers might especially be interested in Craddock's proposal when the subject is so familiar that its mention might cause the listeners to feel deadened by familiarity. "Oh, the preacher is speaking about love. I've heard so much before. I could better spend this twenty minutes deciding how to plant my garden." The preacher may also consider overhearing as a homiletical posture when the topic is controversial or painful and likely to arouse sentiments that would discourage listeners' attention if the topic were broached directly.

In this mode, the preacher does not put the topic (and ideas about it) directly to the hearer. "These are the facts and you've got to make a decision about them and here is the decision I think you should make." Instead, the preacher creates a "situation, or mood, or 'dwelling place' for the participants."[21] The sermon then presents the key themes pertinent to the topic in forms that allow the congregation to "listen in" as these themes are discussed. These forms allow the listeners to maintain a safe *distance* from the discussion. The speaker is not coercing them. Yet because they are free to "reflect, accept, reject, resolve," the community *participates* in the sermon.

A story told in the third person is a classic example of a form which allows overhearing: "There was a certain person. . . ." However, Craddock is far from suggesting that sermons whose intent is to be overheard should always and only be stories. "Communication may be narrativelike, and yet contain a rich variety of materials: poetry, polemic, anecdote, humor, exegetical analysis, commentary."[22] The listeners hear other people in conversation.

Craddock stresses that the preacher creates the sermon entirely for the experience of the hearing community. In *Paradise*

Lost, for instance, "Milton has not structured a statement to let the reader know where Milton stands on creation, sin, freedom, and salvation." Of course, these are "in the poem" for any readers who choose to keep their distance, "but the informational dimension of the poem serves another purpose: the conversion of the reader." [23]

In a sermon that seeks to help the congregation recognize its own small-mindedness and legalism and repent, the preacher would not say to the people, "You are small-minded and legalistic and you need to repent." Instead, the preacher might talk about the phenomena of small-mindedness and legalism, tell stories from other congregations that bespeak the phenomena (and in which the congregation might recognize its own attitudes and behavior). The sermon might sketch an image that pictures the positive changes that happen in a community when the community abandons petty thinking and rigid behavior. The preacher does not "saw the air" and put the listeners on the spot with the condemnatory "You!" Rather, "to deliver a message for overhearing, the speaker will need to trust fully in the message to create its own effect," allow the listeners to exercise their "own freedom, and trust the process, however fragile and accidental it may appear, to be powerful." [24]

As the preacher moves into the design phase of the sermon, other matters come into play as well. What questions need to be asked most fully in this sermon? Which of the hopes and fears of the congregation does the minister take into account and how should they be handled in the sermon? Which of the hearers' cherished values is the sermon challenging or confirming? Can the preacher make use of the material generated in step 2? How can he or she "package" the results of the biblical, historical, theological, and extra-theological analysis so that it can be understood and processed by the congregation? Does the sermon need to deal with the "opposition case" uncovered in step 13? Will the exercise of the imagination in step 10 feed material into the sermon itself? Is the sermon in danger of taking cheap shots at those who hold viewpoints that differ from that of the preacher or the church?

Throughout, the pastor wishes to encourage the sympathetic identification of the listeners with the topic. At the same time, the preacher wants to respect the freedom of the congregation and to avoid manipulation.

Conclusion

This series of steps may seem lengthy, artificial, and cumbersome. Therefore, I close with a rejoinder. Students who have used this process in preaching class at Christian Theological Seminary and who later use it in full-time parish ministry report that it goes much faster than they expect, especially as they adapt patterns of sermon preparation to their own personalities and ministerial life-styles. The preaching of the gospel calls for our best efforts. A topic of importance and controversy deserves a thorough consideration. In any case, one can never predict when the joy of discovery will transform an act of routine study into a moment of shimmering insight.

CHAPTER FOUR

SOME FORMS
FOR THE TOPICAL SERMON

IN THE LAST TWENTY YEARS, THE DISCIPLINE OF HOMILETICS HAS given ever-increasing attention to the form of the sermon. Form, we now know, is not simply a container of meaning (much as the tall glass is the container of a milkshake) but is a part of the meaning itself. Indeed, the experience of hearing the sermon is a part of the message.[1] When the form of the sermon is congruent with the purpose of the homily, the homily has a much better opportunity to accomplish its purpose than when form and purpose work against each other.

A form for the sermon frequently evolves naturally out of the process of preparing the sermon. But at other times the preacher is stymied as to how to shape the sermon and so must search for a form. In either case, the preacher needs to make a critical evaluation of the form to see that form and function work together.

This chapter discusses six possible forms for the topical sermon. Of course, the number of forms for the topical sermon is limited only by the preacher's imagination. I offer these as models which might either give shape to specific sermons or spark a preacher's imagination to adapt or create a shape. These forms (and others like them) can easily be adapted for direct or indirect approaches to the sermon (as described in section 18 of the previous chapter). (The forms illustrate both deductive and inductive approaches as discussed in chapter 1.)

Before proceeding directly to the forms themselves, I want to comment on introductions and conclusions. In several of the following structures, introductions serve similar purposes, as do conclusions. Therefore, this single comment can be transferred to many of the approaches (as indicated).

The *introduction* orients the congregation to the topic of the sermon. Thomas G. Long points out that at the beginning of the sermon, the preacher normally enjoys the interest and goodwill of the congregation. Thus, the introduction does not so much need to arouse the congregation's interest in the topic as it needs to focus the congregation's attention. According to Long, the beginning of the sermon establishes an agreement between the preacher and the hearer: the preacher agrees to talk about the topic that is promised in the introduction.[2]

Some common ways of beginning include telling a story that raises the topic, recalling an event that centers in the topic, offering a provocative insight or image that sparks the imagination to consider the topic, musing about the topic (for example, "Have you ever wondered about . . . ?"). However it is structured, the introduction should not be so emotionally overpowering as to overwhelm the listener's ability to follow the rest of the sermon.

Buttrick points out that the best *conclusion* ends the sermon so as to help the congregation continue to consider the topic.[3] The end of the sermon seeks to suggest ways the congregation can transfer its awareness of the topic to the everyday world.

Normally, the tone of the conclusion should be positive. This creates a desire in hearers to continue being aware of the topic (in contrast to a negative conclusion, which may leave the congregation relieved that the sermon is over). Conclusions make use of stories, images, direct admonitions, and other strategies that prompt the community to pack the sermon into its mental traveling bag.

A simple deductive form of description, evaluation, and application

This form immediately orients the listener to the topic, quickly clarifies the preacher's position on the topic, provides for a description and a theological evaluation of the topic, applies the results of the evaluation to the congregation, and concludes. An outline of the form (and the approximate percentage of each of its constituent parts) follows.

a. Introduction (5–15%)

The introduction orients the congregation to the topic of the sermon as described at the beginning of this chapter.

b. Statement of the main point of the sermon (5%)

In a brief paragraph, the preacher states the main point of the sermon.

c. Description of the topic (15–25%)

The preacher gives a description of the topic. If the topic is a personal or social phenomenon, the preacher sketches who is involved, what happens, the extent of the phenomenon, how the congregation encounters it, pertinent information about the origin and background of the topic, feelings and questions that are awakened by the topic. If the topic is a doctrine, the preacher describes how the topic is manifest in the life of the church (drawing upon related background material from history and practice), voices questions that the congregation may raise about the doctrine or practice, identifies feelings that occur in conjunction with the doctrine. In either case, the preacher wants the congregation to have an accurate picture of the topic.

d. Theological evaluation of the topic (15–25%)

The preacher now evaluates the topic using the norms of appropriateness to the gospel, intelligibility, and moral plausibility. In the case of a personal or social topic, the preacher seeks to identify points at which the topic (and the response to it) coheres with (and is incoherent with) the gospel. In the case of a Christian doctrine, the preacher may not so much need to *evaluate* the doctrine as to draw out those aspects of *how* the doctrine focuses the congregation's knowledge of God's love for all and God's will for justice for all.

e. Application (15–25%)

The preacher applies the results of the theological evaluation to the life of the congregation. What are the implications of the evaluation of the topic for the listening community? What do they learn from the consideration of the topic that helps Christian vision and life-style? The application is usually guided by the purpose of the sermon. For instance, if the purpose of the sermon is to increase the congregation's understanding of the topic, the application would help the community identify and remember those things that are most important.

f. Conclusion (5–15%)

The conclusion would function much as the conclusion described at the outset of the chapter.

As an example of how these points would work, a simple deductive sermon on helping the congregation relate to persons with terminal illness could begin with an introduction which orients the congregation to the fact that we all know people who have terminal illnesses. The statement of the main point could articulate how the preacher sees God present in the situation of terminal illness and how the knowledge of God's presence helps the patient, the family, friends, and congregation. The preacher might then describe pertinent personal and interpersonal dynamics (especially fears and uncertainties). In the phase of theological evaluation, the sermon would explore how the knowledge of God's love for each and all causes us to view the patient, our concerns, and our relationship with the patient. In application, the preacher could outline practical consequences of the knowledge of God's presence for those who relate to persons who are dying, being careful to respect the feelings and fears of the community. The conclusion might then encourage the congregation to draw on the strength of God's presence to relate to persons with the terminal illnesses.

This form is well suited for topics that are relatively uncomplicated and that can be described and evaluated straightforwardly. It can serve personal and social topics as well as doctrinal topics. The form does not work well for topics about which the Christian community holds several different viewpoints.

This sermon structure is best suited to those needs, issues, or situations when the community is likely to be friendly to the preacher's position. If the minister's position is antagonistic to the congregation, its announcement at the beginning of the sermon may foreclose the congregation's willingness to consider the rest of the sermon.

This approach is clear and easy to follow. The congregation should not miss the preacher's point. The method helps the preacher with the task of putting the sermon itself together into clearly identified and manageable pieces. This structure gives the preacher a format that can be quickly appropriated when preparation time is short. In addition, the simple deductive form indirectly helps the congregation learn how to describe almost any topic, evaluate it, and apply it.

On the downside, the form itself (with its announcement of the big idea early in the sermon) tends to excise the suspense that often helps hold listener interest. And the preacher can easily use this form in a dull and wooden way. Thus, the preacher may need to give particular attention to keeping the sermon lively and engaging.

A structure based on the Methodist quadrilateral

We usually think of the "Methodist quadrilateral" as a theological method which draws upon scripture, tradition, experience, and reason as the basic sources from which we derive Christian conviction.[4] In addition, it can provide a simple, instructive structure for the sermon itself.

a. Introduction (5–10%)

The introduction to this sermon functions much like the introduction described at the beginning of this chapter.

b. The Bible (15–20%)

What do we learn from the Bible concerning this topic? The preacher summarizes the biblical witness(es) and points to strengths and weaknesses. As possible (within the limitations of time), the preacher should refer to specific biblical texts and not simply talk *about* the Bible.

c. The tradition (15–20%)

What do we learn from the tradition of the church from 150 C.E. to the present day concerning this topic? The preacher summarizes how the topic has been viewed in the Christian community and points to strengths and weaknesses in those viewpoints. As possible (within the limitations of time), the preacher should mention specific figures in the church. This is often a good time to cite the two theologians (investigated in step 6 in the previous chapter) as well as the position of the denomination.

d. Experience (15–20%)

What do we learn from our experience concerning this topic?[5] The preacher takes account of how we actually encounter the topic as well as of the feelings, thoughts, and other symptoms that are a part of our experience of the topic. The preacher helps us see how these contribute to or detract from our understanding of the topic.

e. Reason (15–20%)

What do we learn from our reason concerning this topic? (1) From the standpoint of internal logic, how does the topic (and our responses to it) cohere with what the Christian community otherwise believes? Is the topic consistent with other Christian beliefs? (2) From the standpoint of the contemporary worldview, how does the topic cohere with what we otherwise think to be true about the world and the way in which the world functions?

f. Synthesis (20–25%)

The preacher brings together the norms of the Christian faith (appropriateness to the gospel, intelligibility, and moral plausibility) as well as what we learn from the Bible, the tradition, experience, and reason. The preacher seeks to arrive at a Christian understanding of the topic.

g. Conclusion (5–10%)

The conclusion to this sermon functions much like the conclusions described at the beginning of the chapter.

For instance, a sermon on the significance of baptism might begin with the preacher briefly describing baptism and posing the question of what this act means for the baptized. The pastor would recollect biblical images of water symbolism and baptism. The sermon could turn next to the tradition of the church and to pertinent ways in which baptism has been understood in the church and could highlight the denomination's understanding of baptism (for example, as a sign that assures the believer of the promises of God). The preacher might then ponder what the experience of being immersed (or of knowing that one was sprinkled as an infant) contributes. The preacher could examine how the denomination's conviction is consistent with the heart of the Christian faith and with the degree to which it makes everyday sense that baptism can perform this function. The pastor would then synthesize the salient discoveries from this process into a brief statement of the summary meaning of baptism and offer images of situations in which the knowledge of being baptized makes a positive difference to the community. The conclusion might offer the congregation an image that helps them remember their baptisms in their day-to-day affairs.

This structure is well suited to those needs, issues, or situations which have a long history. It is an especially useful vehicle for preaching on Christian doctrines. When Christian viewpoints on the topic have changed across time and locale, this approach allows the congregation to follow these changes (and the reasons for them) in a natural sequence. The format also eases the process of sermon preparation itself by giving the preacher a pattern within which to file different kinds of insight and information.

The quadrilateral also helps the congregation perceive the real source of some of its beliefs, practices, and assumptions. A community may think that a particular aspect of its theology comes from the Bible and has been a part of Jewish and Christian tradition since the time of Sarah and Abraham when, in fact, the particular aspect came into the Christian family only in the revival movements of the late nineteenth century. Such knowledge can be crucial in helping the congregation gain a sense of perspective on a given topic.

In addition to helping the community think about the particular topic that is the subject of the sermon, the quadrilateral-as-sermon-structure also demonstrates a systematic approach to thinking through a need, issue, or situation, which the congregation can transfer to other topics. It also helps the congregation to develop a model of authority that incorporates the multiple arenas of Christian knowledge. This model honors scripture, but brings the Bible into conversation with tradition, experience, and reason and it brings them all into the service of the gospel itself.

The quadrilateral can be commended when the preacher and the congregation are on a common, positive wavelength for the sermon. The form itself systematically increases the congregation's awareness of the topic. But the structure can also be used when the preacher seeks to challenge the community's perception of the topic. In the latter instance, each part of the sermon allows the preacher to see how that increment can enlarge the congregation's understanding. The incremental approach can be inviting when the preacher takes an exploratory approach. "Let's see what the Bible says about our topic . . . the tradition of the church . . . our experience . . . reason. . . ."

When using the quadrilateral structure, the preacher will want to guard against letting each part of the sermon remain in its own compartment. The dynamic interaction of the sources should be one of the most vital aspects of the sermon in this mode.

A model based on practical moral reasoning

In recent years, theologians have given increasing attention to practical moral thinking. Don S. Browning, who sees the church as a community of moral discourse, applies this concern to pastoral counseling. Browning envisions the counseling relationship as beginning with the client's experience of the problem and moving through attentive listening and critical analysis in the light of the norms of the Christian community to a decision and strategy for implementing the decision.[6] This pattern can serve as a model for the organization of a sermon.

In making this suggestion, I am not advocating group

counseling. Rather, Browning's practical moral reasoning is a pattern that can help preacher and congregation think systematically and critically about a topic.

a. The experience of the topic (10%)

The preacher outlines experiences of the topic. This stage seeks to help the congregation recognize the phenomena of the topic and to begin to define the topic. Where does the topic touch the lives of the members of the congregation? Can the preacher decribe events and circumstances that the listening community can recognize as true to their own experience in the world?

b. Listen to the experience of the topic (20%)

The sermon helps the congregation attend to its experience of the topic so that the community can identify and name that experience. What feelings and behaviors does the congregation associate with the topic? What questions of value and meaning does the topic raise for the church? At what points do the listeners feel discomfort and the need to come to greater clarity? The preacher helps the congregation understand what is at stake in their consideration of the topic.

c. Critical analysis (30–50%)

This is the heart of the sermon. The pastor helps the congregation think critically about the topic and their experience of it and to identify resources that can help them resolve their points of issue with the topic. Of course, the minister will help the community to recognize Christian resources. In addition, the minister may want to help the congregation consider resources from outside the Christian community, including those whose viewpoints and values are different from the gospel. How do these alternate viewpoints compare and contrast with the gospel? In some instances, of course, the Christian community contains differing (and opposing) interpretations of the topic. At what points do these alternate

Christian judgments compare (and contrast) favorably and un-favorably? The minister helps the community to recognize and assess interpretive options so that the community may make a fully informed decision regarding its view of the topic. The pastor measures the topic and our experience of it against the norms of appropriateness, intelligibility, and moral plausibility.[7]

d. Decision and strategy (20–30%)

The preacher helps the congregation see that they must make a decision regarding the topic and their response to it. Which option (as articulated in step *c*) do they adopt? Why? The pastor must sense the degree to which the sermon can be forthrightly confrontational and the degree to which the choice should be put before the community in a gentle but persuasive way.[8] The pastor also helps the congregation meditate on a strategy for living with its decision and (where appropriate) implementing the decision. What does the community need to do next and what are the resources that can help these steps take place?

For example, consider a sermon that seeks to help members of the congregation clarify their positions on capital punishment. The sermon might begin by pointing to the upcoming execution of a criminal and to the ways in which the Christian family is divided over whether to support or oppose capital punishment. The sermon might then help the congregation identify and listen to the concerns and feelings of those involved in the issue and on its various sides (not forgetting the one to be executed). The burden of the sermon would be to sort through these positions in the light of God's love for all (especially for the criminal) and God's will for justice for all (especially as justice is understood in the *Christian* community in distinction from the legal community). If the analysis concludes that capital punishment is contrary to the gospel, the preacher leads the congregation to think of possible strategies that evolve from that decision (for example, do we fast and pray, write letters to our governmental leaders, join the ongoing vigil outside the prison walls, contribute to a legal fund, or work with legislators to initiate legislation to end capital punishment?).

This approach to the sermon is especially useful when the congregation faces perplexing personal and social issues. The community is aware that it must make important choices regarding how it understands the topic and behaves toward it, but it is confused as to what its conclusions should be and even as to how to go about drawing them. Browning's pattern can particularly help the congregation when an issue can be interpreted in multiple (and sometimes incompatible) ways. This format provides exceptional guidance when preaching on complicated ethical issues.

The sermon based on practical moral reasoning helps the congregation come face to face with its own experience of the topic and with how it is affected by the topic. It brings the congregation into consciousness of those factors that help the congregation decide how to interpret the topic. This form also teaches (at least indirectly) a pattern of moral thinking which can be applied to other situations that develop in the world of the congregation.

The preacher may be seduced into expecting too much from a single sermon developed on Browning's model. A counseling relationship, after all, often lasts several weeks (even months) whereas the sermon lasts only twenty minutes. Remember that it is unlikely that single sermons can routinely bring about total repentances of mind, heart, and behavior. Nonetheless, when the purpose of the message is commensurate with the time available for the sermon, this is a very serviceable form.

A general inductive movement

The general conception of inductive movement in preaching cannot be outlined as a formula with suggested proportions in the same way as in the preceding approaches. By definition, a preacher generates a new pattern for each inductive sermon.

Nonetheless, Craddock suggests one pattern that can be adapted from sermon to sermon: recreating in the pulpit the inductive experience of the process of coming to the heart of the sermon.[9] The way in which the pastor developed an interest in the topic, then pursued the topic in questioning, study, and reflection serves as the "outline" of the homily. The major blocks of material in the sermon correspond to the significant moments in the process of preparation. As Craddock says, the listeners take the trip themselves, and in the process experience for themselves its vistas and valleys. At the end they have not so much *heard* a sermon as they have *participated* in one. For purposes of illustration, I provide an outline which follows the experience of encountering and studying a topic.

a.

The preacher recounts the process of becoming aware of the topic. What happened to bring it to the preacher's attention? How did it come to focus in the preacher's consciousness? What questions, issues, feelings, memories, images does it stir?

b.

The preacher traces the process of discovering that the topic is also important to the congregation. Can the preacher describe some vignettes, images, or questions that help the congregation see itself in relationship to the topic?

c.

The preacher "takes the congregation into the study" and together they explore issues related to the topic as well as resources in the Christian house which help the congregation to make sense of the topic. Pastor and people can work together through basic questions and sources. Craddock cautions the pastor not to underestimate the congregation's ability to sponds to the way they think through the issues of daily life."[10] The community can even follow heavy theology if it is presented clearly. The preacher does not lay out a step-by-step argument as much as probe the issue with the congregation. This part of the sermon may have a tensive character as the preacher and congregation wrestle with sources, insights, ideas, questions, problems, and possible solutions.

d.

Using the insights that emerge from the search of the issue in the previous phases, the sermon comes to a resolution. What is a reasonable, Christian way for the community to understand the topic?

The inductive sermon is a utility approach that can result in a satisfying sermon on almost any subject. It is especially well suited to occasions when the issues are volatile.

The inductive approach can be put to good use when the congregation needs to recognize and own unpleasant things about itself. The inductive homily can lead the congregation into such self-discovery, much as Nathan led David to recognize the truth about David's relationship with Bathsheba and Uriah (2 Samuel 12). The inductive approach is also excellent when an imaginative experience is a principal goal of the sermon. And the preacher may want to turn to an inductive form when the subject of the sermon is familiar to the point of being anesthetic; induction can help reawaken the listeners' numbed interest.

Inductive preaching has a suspenseful quality, rather like a short story. Therefore, it tends to hold the listeners' attention and to draw them into the sermon itself. It allows for the sermon to incorporate many different kinds of data in a natural way. It calls forth great creativity from the preacher (and is thus especially satisfying to the preacher).

However, the inductive sermon can be confusing to the listener if the sermon is not carefully put together. Further, inductive preaching is not well suited for those occasions when the congregation needs an approach that is more like a how-to-put-it-together-handbook than like a Monet painting.

Structure in the mode of praxis

As noted earlier, Buttrick speaks of preaching in the mode of praxis.[11] By praxis, Buttrick has in mind sermons that begin with human experience. Praxis moments, according to Buttrick, are limit moments when the community is confronted by significant questions regarding what it should do or be. The praxis sermon addresses fundamental questions of action (what should we do?) or identity (who are we?).[12]

Buttrick sees the sermon as a macrostructure (called a plot) which is formed by a series of interrelated microstructures (called moves). The sermon intends to have a specified effect upon the consciousness of the congregation. One of the easiest ways to understand what Buttrick means by plot and moves is to think of a conversation. A conversation starts at a given point and proceeds to another point. The conversation then moves from question to question and from one block of material or angle of vision to another.[13]

The move is the basic constituent of the sermon. A twenty-minute sermon consists of four to six moves. Each move can be only about four minutes in length and is formed according to a specific pattern: (a) establishing the focus in about three sentences; (b) developing the move; (c) establishing closure in about three sentences by returning in some way to the initial statement. Each move should contain an image, a "picture" of the concern of the move.[14] The following structure illustrates preaching in the mode of praxis.[15]

Move one

The preacher focuses the consciousness of the congregation on the field of meaning within which the sermon will develop and upon the specific subject matter. Buttrick uses a visual analogy. "The introduction swings congregational conscious-ness toward a picture and then picks out of the picture some particular object with which to begin."[16] The preacher may de-scribe the situation which gives rise to the sermon and bring the situation into a particular focus that is of importance to the Christian community.

Move two

The preacher rereads the situation. We contend with our assumptions regarding the topic. How do we normally under-stand the topic? How do we need to understand the topic? What factors have we overlooked that cause us to see the topic in a broader frame of reference? This is a point at which sys-tematic analysis is often revealing.

Move three

The preacher evaluates the situation and the rereading of it in light of the Christian vision and its norms. How does the Christian worldview compel us to view the topic? This is an act of explicit theological criticism.

Move four

The preacher offers a new understanding or a new course of action. The preacher articulates a vision of how things will be different in light of the new understanding or the new course of action. The preacher helps the congregation revise its patterns of thinking and living.

This outline is not a formula to be applied in a wooden way to every praxis sermon. Sermons in the praxis mode can be arranged in an infinite number of patterns, but praxis preach-ing will need to contain a description of the situation and focus on it, a rereading of the situation, an interpretation of the sit-uation in light of the gospel, and re-visioning for the future.

Suppose a community becomes concerned when it learns that more African-American males between the ages of eighteen and twenty-eight are in prison than in college. In move one, the preacher might describe an African-American youth in prison and pose the question of how the youth got there. What factors does the community need to take into account as it considers this situation? Move two rereads the situation in light of the interrelated factors that create a remarkably discouraging environment for African-American youth: racism, poverty, the inability of the school system to win the attention and trust of youth, the pressures on the African-American family, the injustice of the judicial world. This topic is more than a lot of kids getting in trouble. This is a systemic problem. Move three passes the judgment of the gospel over the factors that contribute to the extraordinary delinquency rate of African-American males. Move four envisions a world with a life system free of the denigrations of our present one and points the congregation to things that it can do to join the coming of this new world (such as becoming aware of its own racist tendencies, visiting in prisons, working for educational and legal reform, and the like).

The praxis approach is particularly helpful when the congregation is in a crisis of understanding or ethics. The praxis model can apply equally well to situations that focus primarily upon the individual or primarily upon the community as community.[17] It serves well for situations that call for an interpretation of the situation in light of its place in a larger life system. (For instance, we may initially perceive a topic in a personal frame of reference but a rereading of the situation causes us to see it as a systemic phenomenon.) The praxis possibility can also guide the formation of the sermon when a traditional Christian belief needs to be evaluated.

This approach inherently asks the community to consider how the situation fits into the larger world system of the congregation. The revising also insures that the congregation leaves the sermon with a sense of hope and practical encouragement. The emphasis on images gives the congregation a lens through which to look at the topic, which they can carry with them to help them interpret the topic as they encounter it in everyday life. The fast-moving style of the sermon (a move every four minutes) is well adjusted to current listener attention patterns that are shaped by television.

But the fast-moving style of this structure may not give the congregation enough credit for being able to follow an argument. It is sometimes impossible to do justice to an idea (make a mental picture of it) in four minutes.

A model which focuses on mind, heart, and will

An older homiletical pattern envisioned each sermon as containing a focus on the mind (understanding, intellect), on emotion (feeling), and on the will (decision). The underlying principle is that these are the three factors in self and community that go into making values and decisions. The sermon is designed to speak directly to each of these three components, thus involving the whole of the self.[18]

Sermonic material relating to mind, heart, and will can be woven into the sermon in many ways. However, for purposes of clarity and simplicity, I portray a structure that is organized in block fashion according to these three concerns.

a. Introduction

The introduction is developed much like the introductions discussed at the beginning of this chapter.

b. Statement of the claim of the sermon

If the preacher is taking a straightforward deductive approach, the preacher states the major claim of the sermon with respect to the topic.

c. Focus on the mind

The preacher seeks to help the congregation understand the topic. What is essential for the congregation to know about the topic? Why is this material important? What are the most compelling intellectual factors in coming to a judgment about the topic? What does the congregation need to learn (or to have reinforced) that will help them see the topic as they need to see it?

d. Focus on emotion

The preacher tries to help the community feel the importance of the topic. The sermon stirs the emotions in light of the major claim of the sermon so that the congregation will be emotionally empowered to act on the call to decision in the next part of the sermon. The preacher searches for a story or other vehicle that can bring the topic into the imaginative experience of the community. However, the minister does not want to manipulate the feelings of the congregation or to be trite or sentimental. The sermon strives for the listeners to develop an honest, emotive identification with the topic.

e. Focus on the will

The preacher helps the listening community make a decision appropriate to the nature of the topic and to the purpose of the sermon. If the purpose of the sermon is for the congregation to come to new insight on the topic, this part of the sermon would ask the listeners to adopt the insight. If the sermon urges the congregation to take a certain action, then this part of the sermon asks the congregation to commit itself to taking the action. The minister is concrete and specific. Often, the sermon will portray the favorable results of making the decision.

f. Conclusion

The focus on the will may be the natural conclusion of the sermon. If not, the sermon concludes as described at the beginning of this chapter.

If the sermon is on God's grace, the focus on the intellect would help the listener understand grace as God's unconditional acceptance. The focus on feeling might create an imaginative experience in which the listeners feel unconditional acceptance. The focus on the will would ask the listeners to accept God's grace for themselves and to accept others graciously.

This threefold approach works best in connection with topics which are relatively uncomplicated and on which a Christian viewpoint can be established directly and without much debate. The model is especially useful for preaching on Christian doctrines (as on grace). It urges the congregation to appropriate the doctrine on all levels of the self. The pattern can support sermons that deal with simple personal and social needs, issues, and situations. It is also a good model when the sermon calls for a friendly action, such as responding to One Great Hour of Sharing.

In this model, the preacher has a clearly defined understanding of the function of each part of the sermon. This makes for ease in preparation. The sermon seeks to integrate mind, heart, and will (albeit it considers them compartmentally). It asks for believers to become intentional regarding their beliefs and actions. It should help people who have been divided within themselves on a topic, perhaps feeling one way but acting another, or perhaps experiencing a rift between intellectual commitment and emotional energy.

However, the tripartite structure (mind, feeling, volition) is artificial.[19] In the actual self, these three are not neatly divided as in this model; they function in dynamic interaction. Furthermore, all human beings do not follow the same sequence in coming to decision. Some people feel a topic before they think about it while others make a decision and only later reflect on the reasons for it. Still, this approach can prove an occasional friend.[20]

Conclusion

The current discipline of homiletics is quite diverse and pluralistic in its proposals for sermon form and structure. The relative merits of each proposal are debated. But the pluralism of the current times is a definite advantage for the preacher. Instead of trying to jam every sermon into an invariable formula, the preacher can discover (or create) a form to serve a particular occasion and purpose.

In this chapter we have highlighted some homiletical approaches that suit the topical sermon. Some will prove more amenable than others to a given preacher's style, personality, and theology. Some might fit a particular congregation with the ease and comfort of a well-sized ring while others would be as troublesome as a ring that is too tight or keeps falling off. Some of these approaches could be adapted and reshaped. Others could spark the preacher's creativity. Still other homiletical possibilities will come to the preacher, clothed for the sermon at hand. The important thing is for the preacher to think critically about the approach and the purpose of the sermon so that the sermon will have the best chance to be welcomed by the listeners and to bring them into awareness of the gospel.

CHAPTER FIVE

STRATEGIES
FOR PREACHING
ON CONTROVERSIAL TOPICS

SOME TOPICS ARE CONTROVERSIAL, WITH MEMBERS OF THE CON-
gregation (or of the larger culture) holding quite different
views. The minds and hearts of some in the community may
be so gasoline-soaked that any opposing view is a match
which sets them aflame. Others may be aware of deep-seated
division in the community but may themselves be confused
about the topic. Some may be sensitive to the pain the topic
causes in the Christian family and may be afraid to discuss the
topic. When the topic comes up, they excuse themselves to go
to the restroom.

The preacher can seldom "decontroversialize" such a topic.
However, the preacher can do some things that encourage the
listener to give the sermon a fair hearing. I have already discussed the importance of selecting a form appropriate to the
topic. This chapter will highlight several factors and strategies
that can help create a favorable listening environment.[1]

The chapter does not present a formula that can be applied
in the case of each sermon on a controversial topic, but suggests several approaches which can be judiciously and creatively combined in individual instances. Based on knowledge
of the congregation and on the nature of the particular topic,

the preacher must judge the degree to which the following strategies can serve the moment. For instance, when helping the congregation see the topic in relationship to the gospel (and not just in relationship to the preacher's personal opinion), the preacher may choose to forgo presenting her or his own viewpoint in a forthright way.

A relationship of trust with the congregation

A relationship of trust between pastor and congregation is foundational for preaching on controversial issues. In fact, a study of the communication dynamics in four congregations whose pastors enjoy the reputation of preaching effectively on issues of social justice discovered that the character and goodwill of the preacher contribute more than the homiletical skill of the preacher to the listener's willingness to entertain the preacher's viewpoint.[2]

The congregation tends to believe a pastor is trustworthy when three qualities are evident. (a) The pastor's life-style is consistent with what the pastor preaches. For instance, pastors who call for peace add credibility to their sermons when they behave in ways that are peaceful. (b) The pastor is "people-oriented." People are trusting when they feel loved by the minister. It is particularly important for the pastor to demonstrate acceptance of parishioners as persons when pastor and parishioners disagree over a decision or issue. (c) The pastor performs the whole range of ministerial responsibilities with care and reliability, such as the minister calling regularly in the hospitals and on shut-ins.[3] A relationship of trust between preacher and people does not mean that the congregation will necessarily adopt the preacher's position. But without that relationship, the congregation is likely to ignore the message, regardless of its merits. When pastor and congregation enjoy mutual trust, they can normally weather the discomforts that come with the encounter of controversial subjects. The community stays together for further explorations of the topic. Thus, the best preparation for preaching on a controversial subject is faithful ministry, week in and week out.

Setting the topic in relationship to the gospel, not just the preacher's opinion

The expository sermon sometimes leads the preacher to a controversial subject in which the ideas of the sermon are basically in conflict with the conventional thinking of the congregation. In such cases, the biblical preacher often seeks to help the congregation wrestle with the subject in the light of the text rather than wrestle with the preacher's opinion on the subject. The congregation finds itself challenged by the text instead of the preacher. The listeners are less likely to dismiss the text than to dismiss the personal preferences of the preacher.

The topical preacher does not use a biblical text as the foundation of the sermon. But, as noted earlier, the gospel message itself functions like a text in the topical sermon. Thus, the topical preacher may want to make a move similar to that of the expository preacher by helping the congregation wrestle with the topic in the light of the gospel itself. The preacher structures the sermon so that the listeners find themselves confronted by the gospel and not simply the preacher's opinion.

For instance, suppose that the United States engages in military action in another part of the world. In the process, the United States bombs another nation and its people, killing thousands upon thousands. A pastor concludes that this is contrary to the gospel and decides to preach a topical sermon that interprets this situation in light of the gospel. The preacher might begin the sermon with a basic gospel affirmation and then unravel the situation against the background of the affirmation. Thus, the sermon might move as follows. God loves each and all. That means that God loves us. It also means that God loves those whom we bomb. If we accept God's love for us, then we also accept God's love for our neighbors and we cannot continue to kill them.

In such a sequence of thought, the sermon moves from a commonly accepted theological claim to the application of the claim in the specific instance. The claim is more than the preacher's personal view; it is the faith of the church. For the congregation to go against the claim is to go against their own statement of how they understand God, themselves, and God's purposes in the world.

A positive tone

The gospel itself is good news. It seeks to encourage, to renew, to offer a constructive alternative to the present order. It follows that a sermon on a controversial topic should inherently have a positive character.

The preacher also has an immediately practical reason for developing a positive sermon. Listeners themselves report that they are more receptive to sermons that are hopeful.[4] They yearn for deliverance and for indications of how the gospel can lead to a better world, whereas they tend to be discouraged and unreceptive when the tone of the sermon is largely negative. Furthermore, a sense of hope is essential to the congregation's willingness to change.[5]

This is not to say that the sermon should avoid negative criticism. At times, the preacher must call attention to values and practices that fall short of the gospel. Such criticism may be necessary to help us assess the present situation correctly and to admit our own complicity in the situation. But negative commentary is never an end in itself. Rather, it is a stage on the way to the point where we can see clearly how the gospel offers us hope in relationship to the topic.

Positive images

The importance of images in the self-understanding and behavior of both individuals and communities is a significant theme of homiletics in the last fifteen years. Images "are not mere rhetorical ornamentation; they disclose the models that shape our minds, and set our behavioral patterns with terrifying power."[6] We live by metaphor.[7] Not surprisingly, authorities in homiletics increasingly see an important role of the sermon in creating images that disclose the gospel's understanding of life and behavior. This does not diminish the importance of ideas *as* ideas but helps us see that ideas are most powerful when they are embodied in images.

It follows that a sermon on a controversial topic needs to offer the congregation positive images which portray a Christian understanding of the topic. Likely, the gallery of the listener's mind is already filled with pictures that orient the listener to the topic in a particular way. The preacher who wishes for the hearers to consider reorienting their perspectives must help the listeners change their images. "Images are replaced not by concepts but by other images, and that quite slowly."[8]

Craddock cites five principles for developing images. (a) The best images are drawn from the everyday world of the hearers and are set forth in forms that the hearers can recognize and believe. (b) The best images use language that elicits concrete responses from the congregation, for example, "the odor of burped-up milk on a blouse." (c) The best images use adjectives and adverbs economically. (d) The best images avoid self-conscious and unnecessary interruptions. (e) The best images are spoken in one's own language.[9]

Developing positive images is hard work. It is nearly always easier to scrape negative images of present thinking and acting off the bottom of the trash barrel of life than it is to generate positive images which can lure the congregation into a new world shaped by the gospel. But the simple fact is that the congregation is most likely to move toward a new possibility when they can experience it imaginatively and when they can feel the energizing power of its hope.

Stories

The telling of stories can be important in a topical sermon. If the story is well selected and well told, "the listeners recognize their own lives in the story, their own joy, pain, disappointment and hope, and without being clearly aware of it, they think and feel their way into the story's situation and characters." The hearers identify with the narrative. "Without directly speaking about the listeners, the sermon nonetheless comes across to them as if meant for each of them personally."[10] The listeners empathize with the story, refract it through their own lives, and add it to their reservoir of experience.

Of the many contributions that stories make to sermons, four are of particular value to the sermon on a controversial topic. First, a story can be a positive image. The hearers can imaginatively experience the controversy as resolved in the gospel. They can "try on" the new world and experience its promise. Second, a story can introduce the congregation to the topic in a sympathetic way. For instance, a sermon on racism could begin with a story of an incident in which an African-American encounters racism. The congregation would then identify with the hurt of racism. Third, stories can help make us aware of how the controversy is experienced by those on different sides of it. Fourth, when appropriate to the sermon, a story can help the community envision concrete responses to the topic. A story about the needs of migrant workers, for instance, helps the congregation think of ways they can relate to migrant workers.[11]

The best stories are either drawn from real life or (if composed by an author) have the sense of real life. Stories can be freely imaginative and full of exaggeration and still have the quality of reality if they inspire feelings and recognitions that bespeak the tensions of real life. Trite and sentimental stories only distance the listeners from depths of life and from the gospel itself.

Personalize the topic

The congregation appreciates having the topic brought into their everyday world. The preacher "personalizes" the issue by showing how the topic relates specifically to the listeners. This is helpful on two levels. One level is that of understanding. As one listener said, the preacher "refers to concrete incidents and struggles and talks about how the issue impacts our everyday lives, where we are personally involved in some level or form of the controversy or problem." This "makes it easier to see how we are connected to the issue and where we can plug in."[12]

Another level is that of helping the congregation to identify specific things that they can do about the topic. Congregations have a tendency to feel helpless and immobilized in the face of massive problems and issues. The sense of helplessness gives way to one of empowerment when the preacher suggests concrete actions that the congregation can take in order to address the topic.

Credible support

The preacher's judicious use of credible supporting material makes a positive impact on the congregation. The congregation likes to know the *reasons* for the position the pastor takes on the issue. They are reassured when the preacher is conversant with resources such as psychological or sociological studies. This shows that the preacher has approached the topic seriously, has taken the time to prepare, "knows the facts" on the topic, and is in dialogue with the mainstream of life. The authority of the sermon is thereby increased.[13]

However, the people will react against a barrage of technical information. In the sermon itself, the preacher should cite only that part of the research that is directly pertinent to the sermon and should do so as simply and directly as possible. The worshiping congregation cannot be expected to absorb complex data and conclusions.[14]

Honest struggle

When pastors speak openly and honestly about their own struggles to understand the topic, the people are empowered to struggle with the topic as well. And the fact of the pastor's struggle adds authenticity to the pastor's resolution. The pastor's conclusion does not sound casual and cheap but has the ring of being hammered out on the anvil of human angst.[15]

Listeners report particular appreciation when the pastor tells an appropriate personal story about struggling with the issue. Many times, parishioners hear their own doubts and fears in the pastor's story. The pastor can be a trusted guide because the pastor has walked where they walk.[16]

Low-key introduction

It is usually best to begin the sermon on a controversial subject in a low-key way. This is especially true in two instances. The first is when the topic itself is sensitive or discomforting. The mere mention of the topic causes some listeners to turn away from the sermon and to focus on their own sensitivities and discomforts.

The second is when the preacher's viewpoint goes against the congregation. If the preacher opens the sermon with the main point of the sermon, the listeners tend to become defensive. Instead of following the rest of the message, they silently develop their own rebuttals, thereby only reinforcing their own viewpoints. (I once heard an elder at the Lord's Table offer a prayer that systematically refuted every point a preacher had just made in a sermon.)

A low-key introduction often helps the congregation make a commitment to stick with the sermon. The preacher might ease into the topic with a human story, with questions which raise the topic in a gentle way, with a description of the pastor's own dilemma about whether or not to preach on the topic, with a description of a scene in which the congregation can recognize itself, with a friendly analogy from which the preacher can move naturally into the topic. The preacher may want to begin with a crisp discussion of the theological premise that underlies the sermon. In any case, the preacher wants to avoid firing an opening shot which leaves the congregation dead to the rest of the sermon.

Forthright pastoral viewpoint

The sermon on a controversial topic normally calls for pastors to make a forthright statement of their own viewpoints on the subject. This is partly a matter of pastoral integrity. But it also works to an advantage in communication. A study of hearers finds that they want to know what the pastor thinks (and why the pastor thinks it) and that they are frustrated when they do not know the pastor's judgment. Listeners tend to mistrust a preacher who is unclear. Even when members of the congregation disagree with the preacher's viewpoint, they tend to respect the preacher and to give serious consideration to the viewpoint when they know where the preacher stands and when they sense the goodwill of the preacher toward them.[17]

Sometimes it is impossible to come to a definitive interpretation of a controversial subject. The pastor holds a preferred interpretation, but this judgment is provisional. This, too, should be acknowledged plainly. We wish to speak with confidence tempered by the humility which comes from the recognition that we are finite and that our judgments are sometimes quite relative. The call to clarity extends to those occasions when the pastor feels compelled to say something about a topic but cannot decide what to say. Public acknowledgment of the pastor's uncertainty may give the people permission to name and claim their own uncertainties. This is honest; it adds to the credibility of the preacher; it avoids coming to a premature conclusion; it also gives congregation and leader a free space in which to think further about the implications of the gospel for the topic.

Recognize and respect congregational understandings

The congregation wants to know that the minister understands what they think and feel about the controversial subject. They are likely to keep the doors of their minds and hearts open to the sermon if the preacher sends the congregation a signal that she or he understands them. The community is less likely to dismiss the sermon if they feel that the preacher does not dismiss them.

The preacher can communicate this understanding in many ways, such as stories in which the community can hear itself, questions the community asks about the topic, direct reference to congregational thoughts and feelings, or allusions to the community's experience of the topic. It is important for the preacher to show respect for the congregation's attitudes and emotions, especially when the preacher is encouraging the community to change.

Present all sides on the issue

Almost by definition, a controversial subject has different sides. The preacher who presents the different sides in a sermon adds to the credibility of the sermon. This creates the impression that the preacher is honest. It communicates that the preacher has investigated the issue in a thorough and fair way. It suggests that the minister does not prejudge the issue but is open to other opinions. It lessens the likelihood that the congregation will experience the sermon as propaganda. It allows members of the community who hold positions other than the one commended by the pastor to feel recognized. It enhances the listeners' sense of freedom by reminding them that they are not prisoners of one interpretive option. This all increases the likelihood that the listeners will seriously consider the possibility that the preacher poses in the sermon.[18]

One researcher discovered that it is helpful to present one's own conclusion *after* presenting the viewpoints of others. Listeners are more open to a change of mind if the viewpoint they support is stated in the sermon. This releases tension. When the congregation believes that their position has been given a fair hearing, they tend to hear other positions with a relatively open mind.[19]

Name resistance

The psychologist Roger Fallot suggests that preachers adapt a notion from psychoanalytic theory to help deal with resistance from the congregation toward a controversial topic. Instead of viewing the congregation as adversaries, the minister regards the community's resistance to a topic as "intelligible misgivings." This shift in perspective encourages the pastor to want to empathize with the listeners and to "understand the complex feelings and ideas likely to be generated by a particular topic, and to anticipate the probable forms resistance may take."[20]

The preacher deals with resistance by addressing it directly. In the sermon, Fallot recommends that the minister explicitly acknowledge the congregation's resistance to the subject and clarify the feelings that accompany it. Such empathetic response to the congregation's resistance may help the congregation be more likely to explore the controversial issue. For instance, a sermon asks the congregation to consider how they use their wealth. But an upper-middle-class congregation may not think of itself as wealthy. In the sermon, the preacher meets this resistance by sympathetically naming this block. "We always think of the rich as them . . . but if we are honest with ourselves . . . ." Some common types of resistance are denial of the reality of a controversial situation, minimization of its importance, or avoidance of knowledge about it.[21]

A realistic expectation for the sermon

Preachers render a service to themselves and their listeners by having an expectation for the sermon that is proportionate to what can realistically transpire as a result of a twenty-minute sermon. When a topic is lodged in a web of thick and entwined values, feelings, and long-standing practices, a lone sermon is usually insufficient to bring about a complete transformation of thought and behavior. Changes in worldview usually occur in incremental stages.[22] It is normally unrealistic for preachers to think that they can step into the pulpit with a cold topic and generate enough heat in one sermon to melt the polar icecaps in the hearts and minds of the listeners.

But a sermon can encourage an incremental change proportional to the present status of the congregation and the time available for the sermon.[23] If the purpose of the sermon is to increase the congregation's knowledge about a topic, the preacher can assess the width, breadth, and depth of the congregation's current knowledge base, and think of a reasonable knowledge increment that a sermon could add to that base. The preacher might ask, "How large an image can I hang in the gallery of the community's mind?" This relieves the preacher of the burden of unfilled expectations and it relieves the congregation of the enervation of being asked to do more than they are ready to do at a given moment. Thus, patience is a friend to the preacher who addresses controversial issues. An established pastor can ordinarily take a long view and regard a given sermon as contributing to an ongoing series of encounters on the topic.[24]

Articulate questions

Listeners report that they respond favorably when the preacher articulates questions about the topic, particularly questions that linger in their own minds. The preacher becomes a "questioning listener" who listens to the questions of the community and represents those questions in the sermon.[25] One study found that the listeners valued the questions raised in sermons as much as they valued the conclusions offered by the preachers.[26] This helps the congregation find themselves in the sermon.

The preacher can also use questions as a nonthreatening way of leading the congregation to consider the topic or a specific perspective on it. "How do you imagine you would feel if you were living under apartheid?"

However, Hans Van der Geest warns against designing the sermon as a two-part movement from questions to answers. The first part of the sermon typically portrays questions (and the situations in life from which they arise) in gripping ways that arouse deep feelings. "But the second part of such sermons is almost always strikingly bland."[27] Unless the preacher can picture the gospel "answer" with power and vividness to balance that of the questions, the preacher is better off voicing questions as they naturally emerge in the unfolding of the sermon.

Stand with the people

The priesthood of all believers affirms that the preacher stands with the people in need of the gospel's insights into the controversial topic and its relationship to the community. The preacher is not over and against the listeners. To be sure, the minister has a particular function in the body: the minister represents the community (and the gospel in the midst of the community). The minister is charged to teach the gospel in the church. But the representative role does not exalt the preacher above the congregation. The pastor is one with the people under judgment and in need of grace.

The sermon on a controversial subject is strengthened when the pastor communicates this solidarity with the people. They respond positively to the clues in the sermon (and in the whole of the pastor's life) that the pastor is *with* them. These clues include preaching confessionally, mentioning one's own doubts and struggles in the sermon, referring to experiences that pastor and people share, speaking so as to show that ministers include themselves in situations under judgment and in need of hope.[28] On the other hand, the people may feel distanced from the sermon when the preacher "lords it over" the congregation, scolds the congregation as if they were children, speaks disdainfully or arrogantly. The preacher can speak with authority while communicating oneness with the community and not putting down the people.

Avoid deriding and inflammatory language

The pastor should avoid deriding the congregation for two reasons. First, it is inappropriate to the gospel. Second, the "putdown" distances the listener from the speaker and from the message.

Further, the preacher should avoid inflammatory language. This is language that evokes such a torrent of feeling that hearers can no longer think clearly or objectively about the topic. A liberal preacher opposing a contemporary evangelical position commits language arson when heatedly describing evangelicals as narrow-minded, legalistic, self-righteous, woman-hating bigots. Such language, as Kelly Miller Smith puts it, sends people out of the pews and onto the ceiling.[29]

Each congregation has its own combustion points, which pastors can discover through careful listening. With creativity and forethought, a preacher can speak the truth without resorting to pyrotechnics.

Humor

A preacher can sometimes use humor in a sermon on a controversial issue.[30] Humor can help the people see the topic in a new but nonthreatening way. It can function as a tool for self-discovery by letting the congregation reevaluate its relationship to the topic in a relatively painless manner. It can provide moments of relief in the midst of considering a heavy topic. It can reveal the ludicrousness of certain views of the topic or responses to it. If it honors the integrity of the listener, humor can help the congregation relax and lower their defenses.

The best humor is not the canned joke. (Canned jokes are rarely a hit, anyway.) The best humor usually comes from the incongruities and surprises the preacher notices in the relationship of the congregation (or the preacher) with the topic.

The use of humor requires circumspection. The preacher never makes laughter at the expense of other persons. The preacher never uses humor as a cover for dealing with an opponent (or an opposing view) in caricature. The preacher never uses humor so as to cause a congregation to take a serious issue too lightly. The pastor never cheapens a poignant experience or insight with inappropriate humor.

Warm and engaging delivery

Listeners respond positively to sermons that are delivered with warmth and energy. In fact, if the sermon is not delivered in an engaging way, the congregation tends mentally to switch to another network. The congregation interprets the following as among the qualities of engaging delivery: The preacher does not read the sermon, but "talks" it. The preacher's body posture is open and accepting. The people can hear the preacher clearly and the preacher's voice patterns are similar to those that the preacher uses in ordinary speech (that is, the preacher does not have "pulpit voice"). The preacher has eye contact at key moments in the sermon. The preacher's facial expressions, gestures, and tone of voice are lively. All aspects of delivery should be commensurate with the personality of the preacher.[31]

One of the worst things a preacher can do is to deliver a sermon on a controversial topic in an angry way. A pastor's anger devastates the communication process when it is directed at the congregation. A preacher also disrupts communication when speaking angrily about someone outside the immediate preaching situation (such as the architects of United States policy toward Central America). Listeners tend to experience such anger not as righteous judgment but as the preacher venting hostility in an inappropriate forum. They feel more defensive than penitent. Anger, so expressed, works against the gospel witness of love and justice.[32] In any case, Walter Brueggemann points out that grief and mourning are usually more adequate expressions than anger to convey the depth of human response to injustice[33] and, by extension, to many other controversial matters.

This is not to say that preachers should not talk about their feelings of anger toward God or about a situation. Pastoral honesty may sometimes call for this very thing, but the preacher can talk about being angry (and can do so with some intensity) without "blowing off" in the pulpit.

Feedback

Communication theorists stress the importance of feedback to a speaker.[34] By receiving adequate feedback, speakers can evaluate their speeches; they can build upon their successful strategies and strengthen the points at which they do not communicate as well as they wish. During a live speaking situation, a sensitive speaker can "read" the feedback of the audience and adjust the message accordingly. Preachers typically receive feedback from their own observation of the congregation during the sermon, at the door, from an occasional parishioner who intentionally contacts the preacher regarding the sermon, or possibly from a formal "feedback" group.

Feedback plays an additional role in the case of the controversial sermon. Listeners appreciate an invitation to respond to the preacher concerning the content of the sermon. They regard this as a sign of the preacher's openness and collegiality. The possibility of talking with the preacher also helps the listeners feel less "trapped" by the sermon and as though the preacher respects their freedom. To provide occasions for feedback, preachers can organize formal feedback opportunities, such as discussion groups or educational events, or indicate their openness to talking with parishioners about the matter.[35]

Sermon a part of systematic consideration of topic

A sermon on a controversial topic will frequently have its best effect if it is part of a series of ways in which the topic is addressed in the life of the congregation. Those who study congregational life are continually reminding us that a congregation is a system in which all parts function together.[36]

The sermon on the controversial topic is not an isolated event with isolated results but takes place in the network of congregational relationships and likely will affect those workings. Likewise, the congregational system can help the congregation deal with the topic in more depth and precision and with greater opportunities for dialogue than afforded by the sermon alone. The church might sponsor a forum after the service, or organize a study group or task force, or bring in a panel of persons to discuss the topic, or provide literature, or devote a fellowship meal to the topic, or put together a work project, or hold a retreat, or devote a quarter of lessons in Sunday school to the topic.

Conclusion

The use of particular communication strategies cannot guarantee that the whole congregation will stay on the wavelength of the sermon. In fact, a recent study indicates that many listeners let disagreeable messages run past their minds. They simply may not hear the message or they may even distort the message to conform more closely to their beliefs.[37] (This accounts, at least in part, for those occasions when pastors take a risk by saying things that they know are antagonistic or painful to the congregation only to see the congregation smile through the sermon and then shake hands at the door saying, "Nice sermon, Reverend."[38]) The use of the approaches described in this chapter may help the sermon get inside the consciousness of the hearer, but cannot guarantee it.

The preacher cannot assume responsibility for the many ways in which members and friends respond to a sermon on a controversial subject. The preacher's responsibility is to prepare carefully and to try to open the door of the topic so that the congregation will want to come into the world of the sermon. The preacher should respect the freedom of the listener (who, after all, has the right to say "No"), even while maintaining his or her integrity and that of the gospel itself.

When the controversial sermon seems to fail (a judgment that cannot always be made close to the time of delivery), the preacher's best response may be to remember that God is the author and guarantor of the gospel, to acknowledge one's finitude, and to commend the congregation to God in prayer. The preacher can then get on with preparing the sermon for the next Sunday.

CHAPTER SIX

SAMPLE TOPICAL SERMONS

Two questions nearly always come up when a homiletical theory is presented to a group of pastors. (a) "Will it work?" In practical terms, can we use it to prepare and preach sermons that the members of our churches will find meaningful? (b) "How do you do it?" Can you point us to examples of this homiletical approach in action?

This chapter provides examples of topical sermons. The sermons were preached in actual congregational settings. Each sermon is briefly annotated to indicate selected points at which the sermon is instructive for topical preaching.

The first sermon focuses on a need from an individual perspective, the second and third center on doctrinal matters. The last sermons offer topical examinations of contemporary issues (homosexuality, abortion).

Forgiving and Letting Go, **William J. Wassner**

William J. Wassner is pastor of Westview Christian Church (Disciples of Christ), Indianapolis, Indiana. He is a graduate of Texas Christian University, the University of Chicago Divinity School, and Christian Theological Seminary.

*This sermon deals with the need of individuals to practice for-
giveness. The preacher draws upon the Christian doctrine of forgiveness and applies that doctrine to everyday relationships.*

Not long ago, I conducted an "unscientific survey" among
our members to find out some subjects about which you would
like to hear sermons. A clear majority asked me to preach on
the topic of forgiving one another.

*The preacher immediately reminds the congregation that they
have reason to be interested in this sermon.*

Forgiving one another is important in the Bible and in the
church. In Matthew, Jesus says that if you are at the altar (we
would say the Lord's Table) and remember that someone has
something against you, leave your gift and go to them and be
reconciled (Matt. 5:24). Every Sunday we pray as Jesus taught
us, "Forgive us our debts, as we forgive our debtors" (see
Matt. 6:12). Peter asked him, "How many times shall we forgive those who do wrong to us?" Jesus replied, "Seventy-
seven times" (Matt. 18:21–22, paraphrase). In Luke, when
Jesus is dying on the cross, he prays that God will forgive the
very people who are putting him to death (Luke 23:34).

The letters of the early church continue the call to practice
forgiveness. The writer of Ephesians says, "Let all bitterness
and wrath and anger . . . be put away from you, . . . and be
kind to one another, tenderhearted, forgiving one another,
as God in Christ forgave you" (Eph. 4:31–32). This call
comes down through the centuries. And right now, one of our
denomination's emphases is to develop congregations that
practice prophetic, redemptive, and *reconciling* ministries. Forgiving one another: as old as Joseph's brothers, as new as
today.

We don't forgive one another just because we are com-
manded to do so. We practice forgiveness because God forgives us. We are forgiven. That's who we are. A part of our

114

identity as Christians is to be forgivers. God forgives us and we respond by forgiving. So when we forgive, we act out who we are.

The preacher draws upon scripture, tradition, and the gospel itself as the theological base for the sermon.

The fact is, we pay a tremendous price when we do not forgive—sleepless nights, guilt, unchanneled and destructive energy, bitterness, even ulcers. But when we forgive, we are set free. We can sleep. We are more purposeful and directed. We even feel better physically.

In my "unscientific survey" I heard you asking two big questions. First, what is forgiveness? And second, how do we forgive?

The word *forgiveness* was originally used mainly in the economic sphere. It referred to release from debt. If I owed you fifty dollars and you released me from that debt, then you forgave me.[1] The word was applied to the sphere of human relationships. In a sense, the forgiving person "cancels a debt" in a relationship. The forgiving person removes all binds or hindrances to the relationship. The forgiver and the forgiven can start their relationship afresh.[2]

The preacher does not assume that the congregation understands the meaning of forgiveness. Here and in the following paragraphs, the preacher helps the congregation get a clear picture of its meaning.

Something happens in a relationship to cause you pain. Someone says something or does something which hurts you. You cannot shake it. It haunts you. You know this is not what God wants. In fact, this broken relationship may be like a pothole in the highway between you and God.

In my reading, I discovered that forgiveness usually takes place in four stages.[3] First, you see the other person and the relationship as valuable. You see that God loves the other as much as God loves you and that God wants you to live together in support and encouragement. God does not want you to live in pain.

Second, you resolve to stop blaming the other person. A professor at a theological seminary says, "Blaming seeks to finger the culprit, assign the role of villain, and proceed to exacting a commensurate punishment. (All of which are negative, alienating acts that increase rather than reduce distance.)"[4] You recognize that blame is only pushing you further apart, so you resolve not to do it.

Third, you decide to go to the other person and try to work it out. You decide that you do not want the hurts of the past to rule the present.

Fourth (and this is the hard part), you go to the other person. Forgiveness is an intentional act, something you do. Of course we don't go alone. God, who is always present with us, goes with us to strengthen us.

Psychologists who study forgiveness say that it is very important for both parties to listen to the feelings of the other. You tell the other person that you love him or her. You explain that you were hurt, but that you don't want the hurt to stand between you. You indicate that you are letting go of the past hurts and that you want to trust the other person in a new future. A new start.

Yes, there are uncertainties in this new start. Yes, there is an element of risk in making it. Yes, you might hurt me again. (I might hurt you.) But I am ready to trust and risk. I invite you to join me in this new beginning.

And you listen to the other person, to the feelings, the thoughts of the other. She or he may have perspectives that help you both understand the situation better.

We sometimes hear people say, "Forgive and forget." But someone has pointed out that we may not be able to forget. "A man does not forget that his father abused him as a child. A woman does not forget that her boss lied to her about her future. You do not forget that a person you loved has taken cheap advantage of you. . . . "[5] We may not forget, but when we forgive, we determine that past wrongs are not going to run the present or the future. We let go.

Of course, there is no guarantee that because you go with forgiveness to the other person, she or he will respond in kind. She or he may turn you away. In fact, the other person may have died. But . . . but, you can still forgive. Maybe you can't talk to the other directly, but you can still forgive. You can still let go. The relationship may not be restored, but you can bring peace to your own heart knowing that you have done all that was possible for you to do.

After describing the practice of forgiveness, the preacher offers a developed story, which functions as a positive image of the sermon's major point.

I know of someone from another city who had to forgive and let go in his own life. He told me I could share his story with you.

By mentioning that the friend has given permission to share his story, the preacher signals the congregation that he is not violating confidence. By mentioning that the friend is from out of town, the preacher discourages the congregation from wondering about the identity of the person.

His father was abusive and under a lot of stress from sporadic employment and five children at home. The father provided for the family's basic needs and tried to do his best, but he was not a good parent. My friend says, "I forgave my father long ago. While I remember what he was like in my childhood, it no longer has a lot of power over me. I could not say the same for my mother. Inside I was angry at my mother for letting my father abuse us."

My friend's parents separated last fall and my friend said he was happy for his mother. "I thought she was ready, finally, to

117

stand on her own two feet. Then, she moved back into the home with him, and I was filled with anger again. Several weeks ago, she called, and I gave her both barrels. I left nothing in the trash can after I had dumped it on her. You see, I thought that I had 'forgiven' her but I had never let go of a thing. On the phone, I reviewed the long list of crimes my father had committed against us kids. I have a mind like an elephant and I didn't miss a beat."

The phone call ended unhappily. My friend thought back over his young life. "I thought about how difficult it must have been for my mother—to be young and inexperienced, to be insecure financially, to be unsettled, to have five children. Because of my own experiences with children I realized that parents make mistakes. (For most of us, parenthood is kind of like on-the-job training.) I realized my mother had her reasons to stick it out with my father. My parents are in counseling now, and it is taking a lot of patient and forgiving love for them to work through the past. But they are letting it go. I realized that even though I resented my mother's choices in the past (and I still don't think they were the best ones), I need to let them go, too."

In this image, the preacher acknowledges the damaging character of abuse and implies that abusive relationships should not be tolerated. But he also acknowledges that it is possible to work toward healing damage from past abuse.

My friend says that he could think of little else for days. "Finally, I picked up the phone. I told my mother that I was sorry. I told her that I loved her and that I forgave her for whatever mistakes she had made as a parent. I told her how much I appreciated the things she had done right, too. I asked her to forgive me, and she wept and said, 'Yes . . . yes . . . yes.' We cried and talked and cried and talked. It was as if a tremendous burden was lifted off my shoulders. I'm sure I will remember the past again, but I do not think it will control me like it did."

You may need to forgive someone today. It may be a co-worker, a neighbor, a friend, a family member. It may be yourself. It may be someone you can't call. It may be someone who has died. But you can do it. You can let go. Even if the other person doesn't reciprocate, you can let go of what stands between you. God wants us to be free. That's why God gives us the practice of forgiveness . . . and letting go.

The preacher concludes by trying to help the congregation relate the central image to their own situations. The conclusion is strong and positive.

Starting a Fire, L. Susan May

L. Susan May was Associate Pastor of First Christian Church (Disciples of Christ) in Vincennes, Indiana, before beginning graduate study at Vanderbilt University. She received degrees from Purdue University and Christian Theological Seminary.

This sermon focuses on evangelism. The preacher clarifies the nature of evangelism, draws upon the gospel itself as the source of the evangelistic impulse and as that determining the character of evangelism. The preacher helps the congregation envision themselves as evangelists.

Have you noticed how there are a lot of religious words that people don't use much anymore? I'm thinking about words such as grace, redemption, justification, conviction, getting slain in the spirit. Some of these good old faith words have been stuck on the back shelf, along with the old hymnals and the blunt pew pencils and a box of matches for the candlelight service.

Let me give you an example of a perfectly good word that many of us are just a little uncomfortable with and don't use much anymore. "Evangelism." Did you draw back just a little, not quite sure you want to come with me down this particular road? Evangelism sounds so . . . zealous. It sounds so . . . extreme. I suspect that many of us hope to keep that word tucked away in the closet at the end of the hallway.

The preacher identifies congregational resistance to the topic. Subsequently, the preacher seeks to help the congregation work through its resistance.

Well, I'm going to tackle this word. I'm going to start from scratch and see if I can figure out just what evangelism is and what it's for. And then we can decide if it is to be kept up there with the moldy hymnals, or if we might just want to take it down, and dust it off, and squeeze a little preaching out of it.

The preacher takes a semideductive approach. She tells the congregation how the sermon will develop but does not reveal the main point.

What is evangelism? I looked up a couple of definitions and this is what I discovered: all the definitions start out the same. "Evangelism is preaching the good news to. . . . " "Evangelism is the proclamation of the gospel so that. . . . " All the definitions agreed that evangelism is telling the good news. It is not just *doing* or *being* the good news. Evangelism is unmistakably an act of communication. It is *telling* the good news.

The preacher does not assume that the congregation understands the meaning of evangelism and so defines it carefully but without technical language.

So far, this seemed pretty easy. I thought to myself, "All I need to do is get up in the pulpit and give you a pep talk to go outside these walls and tell the good news."

But then, I thought I'd better look up some references in scripture. Of course, the first thing that pops up is the Great Commission, "Go therefore and make disciples of all nations . . . " (Matt. 28:19). Well, that is straightforward, but it doesn't say *why* I would want to do it.

So I checked out Acts 1. The risen Christ says to the disciples, "You shall receive power when the Holy Spirit has come upon you; and you shall be my witnesses in Jerusalem and in all Judea and Samaria and to the end of the earth" (Acts 1:8). Empowered by the Holy Spirit. Now, there's something to persuade a person. Not motivated by guilt or duty but by the gracious action of the Holy Spirit.

And what is it that Paul says? "For if I preach the gospel, that gives me no ground for boasting. For necessity is laid upon me. Woe to me if I do not preach the gospel!" (1 Cor. 9:16). More than an obligation. More than inspiration. It sounds like something we are compelled to do.

The preacher evokes several scriptural passages, all of which are important but no one of which satisfies the purpose of this sermon.

And I think this same irresistible power gripped Jeremiah when he cried out, "If I say, 'I will not mention him [i.e., God] or speak any more in his name,' there is in my heart as it were a burning fire shut up in my bones, and I am weary with holding it in, and I cannot" (Jer. 20:9). . . . Evangelism is about a burning fire: the love of God for all the world. Evangelism is telling the good news of a God who loves the world with burning love.

But doesn't God *already* love the whole world? God's love is unconditional. God loves us in any and all circumstances. We don't earn it. God gives it. So, doesn't God love us even if we buy a new VCR for Christmas instead of sending money to outreach? Doesn't God love you and me even if we secretly love going to movies that promote illicit sex? Doesn't God love you even if you don't pray every day? Doesn't God love you even if . . . even if . . . you don't believe at all? Of course. Of course.

Now if God loves you no matter what, why tell the good news?

One Christian leader puts it very simply. You tell the good news in order to make the hidden God visible.[6] And another teacher in the Christian community says almost the same thing in different language when he says that the goal of evangelism is to make manifest the latent church which already exists.[7]

The preacher posits the theological base of the sermon cleanly and succinctly.

Is there a fundamental difference between *being loved* and *knowing you are loved?* An influential Christian thinker, Søren Kierkegaard, answers, "Yes!" He points out that there are two kinds of deceptions. One is believing in what is untrue. But worse is that of not believing in what is true. Kierkegaard asks, is it more difficult to awaken those who sleep? Or to awaken those who sleep and dream that they are awake?[8] One of the most terrible deceptions is to cheat yourself out of love. It would feel the same to you as if you had never been loved at all.

Is there a difference between being loved and knowing you are loved? I will tell you about a time it made a difference to me.

I had been having one of those mornings when everything was going wrong. The alarm clock had been late. My skirt wasn't ironed. The kids argued about what kind of cereal to eat. I remembered that I had to stop and get gas on the way to school. The pressure began to build, and my impatience grew.

I don't remember now whether it was that one more trip to the bathroom, or the spilled cup of juice, or the lunch box that broke open at the last minute. Something pushed me past the breaking point, and I began to yell. I yelled and screamed. Me, a college-educated, sophisticated, civilized, mature, training-for-effective-parenting me.

I was horrified and embarrassed, completely aware that I was making a fool of myself. But I couldn't stop. Until my daughter came across the room, put her hand on my arm, and said, "Mom, maybe you forgot that we love you."

The juice was still on the floor. We were still late. But that reminder was enough to get me centered and going again.

The preacher uses an everyday story to provide an image of the distinction between being loved and knowing that one is loved.

To know that you are loved makes a difference in your life. When you realize you are loved by God, it's much the same as the feeling of romantic love. When you are in love and you know your love is returned, you want to shout it from the rooftops. You want to tell everyone. It's just burning in you.

So, for my part, I'm all for evangelism. I think we should get it out of the closet, dust it off, and strike some gospel sparks. It's more than church growth. It's more than life-style. It's active, not passive. It's for the dreamers who do not even know they are asleep.

Go ahead. Try it. A little good newsing. Spreading some love around. We've got nothing to lose but pride. And we might, we just might, get a fire started.

What's All This Born Again Business?
Richard L. Lancaster

Richard L. Lancaster was formerly adjunct professor of preaching at Christian Theological Seminary. For more than twenty years he was pastor of Meridian Street United Methodist Church in Indianapolis. He is a graduate of Ohio Wesleyan University and Yale Divinity School.

He examines what it means to be born again in light of the gospel and the teaching of the denomination of which the congregation is a part. Toward the end of the sermon, he uses his pastoral consideration of this issue to give the congregation an opportunity to think about a larger concern.

These days we bump into the idea of being "born again" in so many different places. On television, we hear the born-again testimony of political, athletic, and rock music celebrities. In popular magazines there are articles about booming evangelical churches.

I gather that while this topic does not provide strong feelings for most of us here, it does provoke curiosity and a measure of uneasiness. For some of us, the uneasiness rises out of our uncertainty as to how we ought to identify ourselves; we're not sure whether our understanding and experience of the Christian faith puts us inside or outside the born-again camp. For others, the uneasiness rises out of our certainty; either we are sure we are in the born-again group (and are suspicious of any of our churchmates who are not) or we are sure that we are not in that camp (and are suspicious of any who are).

For us—a single United Methodist congregation on the north side of Indianapolis—is it an "out there" issue or an "in here" issue—or is it some of both? At the very least, we can think about it together and different ones of us can decide where we fit on the spectrum.

The preacher introduces the issue and sympathetically identifies several viewpoints which are held by members of the congregation. This gently names resistance and invites all into the world of the sermon.

Let me start with this: while many of us might not be able, or even want, to call ourselves born again (as that phrase is ordinarily used these days), I think nearly all of us can properly call ourselves evangelicals. Some people who write articles about the booming evangelical churches would say that the typical United Methodist congregation can no longer be called an evangelical church.

Well, I am willing to let those who wish to shut me out of the born-again camp do that if it gives them satisfaction, but I am not willing to let them shut me out of the ranks of the evangelicals. Words such as *evangelical, evangelism,* and *evangelist* all come from a Greek word meaning "good news." That implies that everyone who sees the central message of the Christian faith as good news is an evangelical.

The preacher helps the congregation reread the notion of what it means to be evangelical.

My impression is that most us here *do* see the central message of the Christian faith as good news. I mean by that that if we were to explain to a stranger what lies at the heart of the Christian faith, we would not begin by saying, "I am here to tell you what God wants us to do." Instead, we would begin by saying, "I am here to tell you about what God has done." In Jesus Christ, God has given us a sign that makes it possible to interpret our lives and the whole cosmic story in terms of hope and joy. That is the central message of the Christian faith, the fountain from which all else flows. That is good news. And since seeing the essence of the gospel as good news is what makes a person an evangelical, most of us are evangelicals.

Now for point two: if the Christian faith is going to be real to us, we must move from secondhand faith to firsthand faith. When children are baptized in this church, one of the questions we ask the parents is, "Will you endeavor to keep these children under the ministry and guidance of the Church until they, by the power of God, shall *accept for themselves* the gift of salvation?"

We may grow up in a home where the language of faith is almost part of the air we breathe. But if that faith is to be authentic for us, then somewhere along the way that family faith needs to become *my* faith—something *I* have examined, something that makes sense to *me*, something *I* believe. This is the question you and I must answer: Have I made my own decision to understand myself and the world in the terms of the Christian faith? Have I moved from secondhand faith to firsthand faith?

We're now ready for point three. This movement from secondhand to first-hand faith can take place in several different ways. Sometimes it occurs very suddenly and dramatically. It is like being blind one moment, and then suddenly seeing. It is like being dead, and then suddenly coming alive. It is like being born again. The experience is so emphatic, so unmistakable that we remember the time and place the rest of our lives.

The preacher now looks at the issue from three different perspectives. Happily, in this case, he can acknowledge the validity of each.

Sometimes the movement from secondhand faith to firsthand faith feels more like choosing which side you are going to be on. You weigh the options and then decide the claim that makes the most sense to you, the one that appeals most powerfully to you. We may or may not be able to pinpoint the decision time, but however and whenever it happens, the feeling is more that of having made a decision than of being reborn.

And then sometimes the whole process of moving from secondhand faith to firsthand faith is so subtle, so gradual, so unconscious that we have no awareness of the process going on within us. It is something like moving from Virginia to Indiana, and for months and years you keep on thinking of yourself as a Virginian. But gradually your roots are going deeper and deeper where you are, and one day some occasion arises that causes you to realize that you now identify yourself as a Hoosier.

For some of us, faith comes dramatically. For some, it is more like making a choice. For some it is a gradual process going on within. Different routes, but they can all lead us to the same faith.

Which brings me to point four. The most reliable indicator that we have taken the good news of the gospel into ourselves is what happens to the quality of our lives as measured from that starting point. What happens in our hearts and lives is the most reliable evidence of the presence of the Spirit, the most certain indicator that we have moved from secondhand faith to firsthand faith.

"Beware of false prophets," Jesus said. "You will know them by their fruits" (Matt. 7:15–16). "Every sound tree bears good fruit, but the bad tree bears evil fruit" (Matt. 7:17). The apostle Paul seems to operate on the same premise. "Do not quench the Spirit," he wrote, "but test everything" (1 Thess. 5:19, 21). "The fruit of the Spirit is love, joy, peace, patience, kindness, goodness, faithfulness, gentleness, self-control" (Gal. 5:22–23).

The same note comes through almost like a drumbeat in the first letter of John. Listen:

—And by this we may be sure that we know [Christ], if we keep his commandments. He who says "I know him" but disobeys his commandments is a liar (1 John 2:3–4).
—By this we may be sure that we are in him: he who says he abides in him ought to walk in the same way in which he walked (1 John 2:5b–6).
—You may be sure that everyone who does right is born of him (1 John 2:29).
—Beloved, let us love one another; for love is of God, and he who loves is born of God and knows God. He who does not love does not know God; for God is love (1 John 4:7–8).

Firsthand faith begets firstfruits in living.

Thus far, the preacher has stayed thoughtfully and carefully within the usual parameters of the topic. In the next paragraphs he asks the congregation to venture with him a step further.

In addition, I think there is more in some of these passages than simple reminders that the quality of a person's faith can be measured by the quality of that person's life. I think that several of these passages suggest that wherever we see beauty and strength of character, we see a sign that God is at work in that life, *no matter what that person may say or think or believe.* "Everyone who does right is born of God." "Love is of God, and the one who loves is born of God."

If we take passages like these seriously, I do not see how we could ever again take quite as seriously some of the hard-and-fast lines that people sometimes draw between believers and unbelievers. If all love is reminiscent of God's love, if the Spirit is at work in everyone who loves, well, that really screws up the standard scoring system, doesn't it? But doesn't it also magnify your sense of wonder at God's goodness and God's glory?

The preacher gently makes it possible for the congregation to enlarge its notion of God's activity in the world.

If it is true that all who love are born of God, if it is true that all who really know Christ have more and more the will to keep the commandments of Christ, then it also must mean that when we are troubled by the quality of our own lives, by our own lack of love, by our fickleness, by our pettiness, then the place for us to go is back to the well. Keep taking fresh drinks from the cup God holds out to us in Christ, so that day by day, year by year, the pockets of resistance in us will diminish as the process of *the* faith becoming *our* faith continues.

How it happens doesn't really matter much—whether it comes as a dramatic experience, whether it comes as a continuing series of little births and rebirths, whether it comes as a decision, whether it comes so subtly that we cannot trace it at all. *How* it happens doesn't really matter. What matters is that it *happens*.

Difficult Choices: The Christian and the Homosexual, Richard E. Hamilton

Richard E. Hamilton is pastor of the North United Methodist Church in Indianapolis. He was educated at DePauw University, The Theological School of Drew University, and Union Theological Seminary in New York.

In the following sermon, he struggles toward a Christian understanding of homosexuality and the church's pastoral relationship with homosexual persons. The sermon was preached in 1978, when the subject of homosexuality and the Christian life was initially discussed in an open way in the congregation. While much has since been said about the subject, the sermon is a good example of introducing a controversial issue.

Let me begin by telling you about three friends of mine. I shall not use their names, but everything else is real.

Roger was a tragic misfit. He did not seem to belong in the tidy world of the church-related campus where we were students. Roger was bright and friendly, though in an awkward way. Roger appeared often at church where he was tolerated but not really drawn into the student circle. On many spring afternoons, he would hang around the athletic fields and training rooms, even though he was not athletically inclined. Once in a while Roger would show up at the fraternity house, though no fraternity ever welcomed him. On a few occasions I talked with Roger about the future, about his good mind and his problems with other people. The day came for me to move on. I never saw Roger again. Then, just when most of us were marrying or moving into those futures we had planned, the word came—Roger had died, at his own hand. I do not know the exact circumstances, but I know at least part of the reason. There have been many who lived and others who have died in Roger's closed-in, ridiculed, fearful world.

Nate lived in a different world: married, a father, unfailingly helpful, gentle, physically strong, at home in the out-of-doors. But Nate and I talked more than once about another side of who he was. He was puzzled and confused by it, sometimes in anguish at feelings he could not explain and could not accept and that conflicted with what he had been taught at home, at church, and through the Bible. I tried to encourage him to talk with others more knowledgeable and skilled than I, but he would not. So, Nate continues to live his double life, one acceptable to his friends and to him, the other a silent, passive but terrible world in which he is hostage.

Leo is a professional. His credentials and achievements

draw the respect of his peers. Years ago, Leo faced the same feelings as Nate, but Leo responded differently. He decided they were indeed who he was. Without a sense of guilt, and within a large circle of friends, he lives in another city: productive in work, a conscientious citizen, active in religion, known by many as a part of the increasingly visible gay community. He does not call attention to his sexual identity, but neither does he attempt to hide it.

The preacher begins with the human face of the issue. This encourages listeners to approach the issue from the standpoint of what it means to people.

What shall I say to my friends when they ask me about my thoughts and feelings (and each one of them has at one time or another)? About being Christian and homosexual? What shall we—you and I together as the church—say? That honest, complex question has sent me through a dozen books, many articles and conversations.

The preacher voices one of the congregation's questions. This invites openness and exploration and does not prematurely raise defenses on one side of the issue or the other. The preacher also recognizes the complexity of the issue and signals the congregation he has studied the issue thoughtfully.

My purpose in this sermon is not to settle the issue. My purpose is to lift the whole concern into the light and air of open, reasonable, faithful reflection. Indeed, the first (and for some the most difficult) step is to approach calmly and openly what for many of us has been unspoken, frightening, and distasteful. We must do so not on the bases of dark, deep wells of misinformation, misjudgment, and feelings whose sources are hidden in the recesses of our beings. We must do so on the basis of shared knowledge and faith. Let me share with you where my journey has taken me, some convictions, and some open thoughts.

The preacher names the resistance and then poses a way to work through it.

One simple conviction is that this issue is complex. It has as many layers as an onion. Anyone who attempts to give a simple response does not perceive the breadth and depth of the questions—human, scientific, religious. To say that is not to be paralyzed by complexity. It is to call for a profound humility and willingness to *listen*, to learn from many corners, and to think with precision about a whole cluster of questions.

A second conviction is that society's judgments about homosexuality have caused immeasurable suffering through the centuries. An example. Under the same stern, fanatical regime which sent six million Jews to the ovens in the 1940s, homosexuals were ordered to wear purple triangles on their arms and were sent to death camps in order to purify the nation. That unconscionable story, though extreme, is not isolated. In the lifetime of every adult here, and as recently as today, attitudes toward people like Roger, Nate, and Leo drive fellow human beings to ridicule and to terrible isolation. It tears families asunder, heaps guilt upon tearful parents, and destroys persons in unmeasurable ways.

Whatever may be points of divergence at other levels, there is no justification for the pain well-meaning people inflict upon others. No reading of the Bible, no theology, nor personal judgment can justify what we have done.

A third conviction is that many of us are uninformed and operate with mistaken assumptions. The form of the title of this sermon illustrates and, inadvertently, could reinforce one such assumption—"The Christian and *the* Homosexual." Homosexuality is not a single, uniform reality. It may develop gradually. Sometimes, but seldom, it may be reversed. It may be expressed in celibacy, in promiscuity, or in long-term relationships. Homosexuality cannot be identified with any particular psychological profile nor with any physical characteristics nor with any mannerisms. And, of course, not exclusively with either sex. Roger, Nate, and Leo have their counterparts in Barbra, Joyce, and Maxine.

Experts estimate that anywhere from three percent to twelve percent of men in this country are homosexual. Most of the studies that I read put their estimate at the lower end of the scale: perhaps five percent if the reference is to long-term orientation. As much as thirty-three percent of the male population has had active homosexual experiences of an occasional nature.

There are two things to note about these statistics. First, a great many people are involved directly in homosexual relationships. Second, though definition could take up all our time, no one (particularly the young) should conclude on the basis of occasional homosexual feelings or contacts that he or she is in the smaller segment of those who have settled inclinations and life patterns.

The preacher briefly offers direct pastoral interpretation of a widespread phenomenon.

The causes of homosexuality are by no means clear. One responsible physician lists seventy separate causative factors.[9] Do not let anyone convince you that the origins of homosexuality are well understood. Professionals of equal credentials vary markedly on their judgments.

Parents need to know that popular theories about parental patterns may or may not be truly causal. It is clear that in many cases, homosexual orientation is determined early in childhood, perhaps even in infancy. Some believe there are chemical or hormonal factors. It is important to listen when Dr. Paul Gebhard, Director of the Indiana University Institute of Sex Research, says, "I have never known anyone who is homosexual by choice."[10] This uncertainty mandates that we be cautious in arriving at ethical judgments and arriving at personal responsibility.

Four years ago, the American Psychiatric Association voted

to remove homosexuality from classification as a psychiatric disorder and to consider it an illness only when the individual involved is in conflict with the fact of being homosexual. However, that change was not made with unanimous consensus.

The judgment of professionals in mental health is not, of course, determinative for the moral and theological choice which the Christian community must make regarding homosexuality. But neither can the Christian community make its judgments apart from the best knowledge available.

The preacher now begins to move toward explicitly theological analysis. The previous data contributes to the discussion in an indispensable way but is not itself the heart of the matter.

Christians properly look to the Bible for direction. The long negative judgment which Christians have passed on homosexuality has roots in the Bible, but I must share with you my own reorientation in understanding those roots as a result of my own intensive examination. I am convinced that we cannot appeal to the biblical material for a few simple, Christian judgments.

The preacher shows respect for the Bible yet speaks of sharing his own reorientation concerning the biblical witness on homosexuality. The latter invites the congregation to consider a new way of thinking about the Bible and the topic but in a nondogmatic way.

Out of the whole Bible, there are only three relevant passages. The single most influential passage is Genesis 19, the story of Lot in the city of Sodom. In that story, Lot welcomes two angels in human disguise into his house. In the night, men from the city demand a kind of gang-rape of the visitors. Their violent intentions violate both the ancient laws of hospitality and of sexual conduct. This is a sign that the sin of Sodom is indeed pervasive. It is important for us to note that the offense was an abuse of others and a violation of hospitality. It was not an abuse of consenting adults. More, it is a sign of the general condition of sin which is the real tragedy of Sodom. Over and over again, the Bible refers to this general, willful wickedness and not a particular form of sexuality as the mark of Sodom.

Leviticus does contain a clear prohibition against homosexuality (Lev. 18:22), but this cannot in itself be normative for Christians. In these very same chapters there are prohibitions against a number of things which no Christian today considers absolute: mixing of grain in the fields, mixing of fabrics in clothing, tatoos, eating of meat with blood, trimming of beards, cross-breeding of cattle, and many regulations concerning heterosexual intercourse. We cannot point to one of these prohibitions as normative for Christians and cavalierly dismiss the rest.

More important for Christians is Paul. Paul includes homosexual behavior as one of the marks of idolatry in Romans 1. Homosexual behavior, in Paul's view, was a mark of rebellion and false worship, along with the other specifics listed with it—covetousness, envy, strife, deceit, gossip, slander. But we no longer accept Paul's judgments as normative in other areas, such as the role of women, the legitimacy of slavery, preference in hair fashions or for celibacy, or a dozen other things.

Jesus never mentions homosexuality. One cannot read approval from silence, but any reference to Jesus must include his consistent, surprising, patient, and loving acceptance of many individuals who were judged harshly by their contemporaries.

The preacher does not just talk about the Bible but deals with specific passages in a straightforward way. This assures the listeners that the preacher is not glossing over the biblical witness.

Summarizing, in this limited number of biblical references, homosexual behavior is judged harshly. It is treated as a violation of heterosexual instincts assumed to be universal. The image is invariably one of physical lust. There is no signal that the Bible recognizes what today's psychology affirms—a very early, exclusive, or dominant sexual attraction to one's own sex—and there is no reflection at all of the mutual and loving total relationship of which some homosexuals speak today.

Christians are left with this biblical treatment. We must evaluate it and join to it insight from other directions to discern as best we are able what faithfulness means on this issue, even as we have done with clearer biblical words, about divorce or possessions, for example. My personal conviction is that the biblical understanding of homosexual behavior is limited and cannot bear the full weight of comprehensive theological judgment on the question today.

The preacher states his own position on this aspect of the topic very clearly and reminds the congregation of the complexity of the issue.

Let me move on to three additional thoughts. First, in light of intense human suffering, Christians are surely called to stand with individuals of homosexual orientation in seeking civil or legal equality. There is no justification for denying access to employment or housing because of sexual orientation. In areas where civil protection has been extended explicitly, such as the Washington, D.C., school system, experience has been good.[11] There are, of course, incidents of abusive or degrading homosexual behavior, but there is no substantial reason to single out the homosexual here. His or her heterosexual colleagues can present no more wholesome a record.

Second, within the church, we need to commit ourselves to a process just beginning, namely, that of meeting the homosexual in our midst as a person, not just as a representative of a problem to be solved or a condition to be judged. God sees Roger, and Nate, and Leo as *persons* and so must we.

It is difficult for many of us to see the homosexual orientation as a whole and mature expression of sexuality. There are significant and, for me, persuasive reasons to believe that homosexuality as an orientation is an incomplete or diverted development. It is one thing to accept homosexuality as the best available expression of sexuality for a particular person. It is a separate thing to affirm it as a sexual stance equivalent in human good to the meeting of man and woman so strongly written into biological reality and so prominent in the biblical and theological understanding of creation and the fullest development of human love.

Many within the homosexual community, for understandable reasons, cry for that affirmation of equivalent good. It is not likely that the church will make that full affirmation in the near future. Living with the request and with a tragically overdue reexamination of its historic position will be a part of our agenda for many years. We have been talking about this issue for some time at North Church, and I am sure we will continue. As we do, we need to relate to homosexuals as persons.

The preacher clearly communicates that this sermon is only part of the dialogue. All in the community will have a chance to contribute.

Third, what should be at hand now is a strong commitment in the church to say our understanding is incomplete, our judgments differ, but we are, each of us, sons and daughters of God. There is room in the kingdom, and in the earthly foyer of the kingdom called the church, for us all.

No one of us has a place here on the basis of our maturity, or purity, or spiritual completeness, or in any other way. We are, every one of us, here because of the *unconditional* grace and love of God. Such a love does not wipe out all distinction as to what is good and what is less good in human life. We are not only permitted, but we are mandated to discern such distinctions and to help one another to the fullest human and spiritual stature each of us can reach. But our acceptability within the body of Christ is not dependent upon how we understand that, or define it, or realize it. We have a place here because of Christ's gracious invitation.

> *This is the theological center of the sermon. It does not offer the definitive Christian judgment on homosexuality as a life orientation. (The preacher has already indicated his judgment that the church is not ready to come to such a conclusion.) But it does speak unequivocally of the place of homosexuals (and of every member of the human family) in the heart, grace, and love of God, and in the church as well.*

An Episcopalian priest shared a moving personal testimony in a religious journal. He spoke from the perspective of one who had been divorced and remarried. Listen:

> The Biblical norm calls for sexual expression within monogamous, lifelong marriage. Homosexuals and I live outside. We can, of course, point to others who live outside as well: those who are rich and refuse to sell what they have to give to the poor; those who do not love their enemies; those who do not feed the hungry. But naming others' sins does not change who we are. . . . We live outside. . . .
>
> In my divorce and remarriage, the church has bestowed on me both dignity and protection. I want the same for my brothers and sisters of the gay community. I want my church to be an advocate for their rights, and a mediator of God's blessings for them.[12]

So do I.

> *The sermon both acknowledges ambiguities in our present situation and offers the congregation a firm place to stand while wrestling honestly and compassionately with the topic.*

Thinking Ethically About Abortion, Jon M. Walton

> *Jon M. Walton is pastor of Westminster Presbyterian Church in Wilmington, Delaware. He is a graduate of McAllister College, Union Theological Seminary in New York, and San Francisco Theological Seminary.*

In this sermon, he wrestles in a fundamental and sensitive way with some of the ambiguities in regard to abortion. He draws upon the notions of our limitations as creatures and stewardship as basic theological frames of reference. This sermon, preached in 1990, is a useful illustration of dealing with a sensitive subject.

Perhaps no issue before us is as controversial or divisive as abortion. I cannot untie its Gordian knot in twenty minutes. But I do want to think with you about some of its complexities from a Christian perspective.

Immediately, the preacher acknowledges the complexity of the issue and sets out a realistic goal for the sermon.

I first encountered the real issue of abortion when I spent a summer as a student chaplain at Presbyterian Hospital in Philadelphia. I visited a young woman. When I asked her what had brought her to the hospital, she said, "I'm here getting an abortion. Just in and out. This is my third time." Sixteen years old. She spoke casually, as if all sixteen-year-olds had been through this experience.

She was street-wise and used abortion as a means of contraception. I was appalled at her values. But I ask you, as irresponsible and cavalier as her attitude might seem, would you want to be her child? Was her decision to abort without any wisdom or redeeming social value?

The preacher begins with a case that is a stereotype of the image many in the congregation bring to the topic of abortion. But the preacher's questions invite the listener to move beyond the stereotype and to think of the case (and others similar to it) in connection with their own lives. The preacher seeks to help the congregation personalize the topic.

The second formative encounter I had with abortion was serving for four years on a genetic abortion counseling team at a New York hospital. This group, composed of geneticists and clergy, counseled couples with problem pregnancies. As a team we reflected on the medical and ethical issues involved in carrying fetuses with genetic disorders to full term or choosing to abort them.

In addition to recounting his history with the topic, the preacher establishes his knowledge of the topic.

A typical case went like this. A couple was referred to our hospital by the mother's obstetrician. The couple had three healthy children. The mother was nearly forty, and as you know, the possibilities for fetal abnormality are higher for older mothers. A test (amniocentesis) revealed that the fetus in the womb had a chromosome pattern that almost always resulted in a fatal blood disease. It would begin with easy bruising and bleeding and end with leukemia, probably before the age of ten.

Initially, the couple denied what they were being told. "How can you be sure these things will happen? Maybe we're different." Soon, the irreversibility of the chromosomal damage spoke for itself, as did the experiences of others who had borne children with the same disorder. They knew they had to decide.

They had three living children to think of, young children who needed their attention and time. An ill child would affect the family dramatically. They asked themselves: what parents who know that they can spare their child suffering would knowingly lead that child directly into circumstances where the child would experience a life of continuous suffering and an early, painful death? It was a terrible decision. But they decided to terminate the pregnancy.

They came to think that they were making a decision between the lesser of two evils. They could either bring a terminally ill child into the world and bear the responsibility of knowing that they could have prevented its suffering (and the disruption of the lives of their other children), or they could terminate the pregnancy, which felt very much to them as if they were taking the life of their child. And what do you think you would have done?

This poignant case, again followed by a question, helps the listeners personalize the topic and feel its complexity.

And what if the mother's life is in jeopardy? Statistically speaking, most mothers choose to abort the fetus if their own health is in danger. But does that make the choice any less significant?

Most people agree that abortion is justifiable in the case of pregnancy resulting from rape or incest. We're appalled by the source of the pregnancy, but what about the fetus? Why is its right to life any less than that of a child who is conceived in love?

Medical technology now makes it possible for us to do something similar to what the Psalmist said God could do: to know the unformed substance of the child even in the mother's womb (Ps. 139:16). Looking into the womb with amniocentesis gives us something like a God's-eye view of the child's destiny. Medical science gives us knowledge without the benefit of divine understanding. How can we make wise, faithful, moral choices crippled as we are by the limitations of our wisdom?

The problem is complex. It begs for clarity, but clarity about the many issues involved is almost impossible to achieve. We want a clear moral choice so that we can do the good. But we cannot attain moral purity in this life. All our choices are compromised by our state of sin. We can make better and worse decisions but we cannot achieve sinlessness. We are human, limited, and therefore we make mistakes. What we can do is to make the best choice available under the circumstances.

Some try to discuss this issue in terms of when life begins. They reason that if we could know when life begins in the womb, then we could have a reference point for terminating pregnancy by abortion. But when does life begin? At conception, at quickening, when the fetus has the ability to feel pain, when brain activity begins, at viability (when the fetus can exist on its own, without its mother)? The General Assembly of our church speaks wisely of the point when life begins when it says:

> [T]he morality of abortion is not a question of when life begins. . . . The modern scientific answer to the question of when life begins is that human life and its reproduction are a continuum. . . . It is ultimately senseless to ask when in this continuum . . . a recognizably human form of life can be found. Human life is never absent.[13]

The fetus is always a human life.

If we are to make headway on this topic, we must acknowledge three things. (1) Life is always present. (2) Our decisions about life and the termination of life always dwell in a gray area and can never be untainted by human sin and limitation. (3) Neither of those conditions absolves us of our responsibility *to* and *for* others.

The preacher has now set the stage for speaking more specifically about the factors that contribute to coming to the best choice available.

So here is how I view abortion. Pregnancy is a condition of stewardship, a trust from God. As in all things, we make the best choices that we can with this trust.

The preacher states his own view clearly.

There are many issues involved, including those of women's justice and a woman's right to control what happens in her own body. But from a Christian point of view, both men and women are responsible to glorify God with their bodies. Our bodies are a gift to us and so is pregnancy. In this respect, to bring a child to full term carries moral responsibility just as much as does terminating a pregnancy.

Of all people who might offer insight into this issue, I want to remember John Calvin, who wrote this about the stewardship of life.

> [God] who has set the limits to our life at the same time entrusted to us its care; He has provided means and helps to preserve it; He has also made us able to foresee dangers; that they may not overwhelm us unaware; He has offered precautions and remedies. Now it is very clear what our duty is: . . . our duty is to protect (life); if He offers helps, to use them; if He forewarns us of dangers, not to plunge headlong; if He makes remedies available, not to neglect them.[14]

Calvin is very clear: our duty is to protect life.

Life is sacred, and it is sacred because of its source, God. But there is a danger in retaining life at all costs. That danger is idolatry, the idolatry of keeping "a person's (or even a fetus's body) alive no matter how empty that life may be."[15] We want to protect life. But we do not want to make an idol of the fetus.

When the fetus is dysfunctional, the decision to continue with the pregnancy or to abort is crushing. I have found myself supporting parents who have faced this decision and who have decided in both ways. Many families who have Down's syndrome children, retarded children, children with Tay-Sachs, hydrocephaly, spina bifida, trisomy, Huntington's disease, and other disorders have often been among the most courageous, close, and blessed families I have known.

But it is not fair to romanticize their situation. Grief is often the constant companion of such families. So for some families abortion seems the better choice.

What about those who use abortion as a means of contraception? Considering the availability of conventional contraceptive devices and the moral gravity of abortion, abortion ought to be the last option for contraception that is ever used. Even so, the truth is that no contraceptive device is 100 percent reliable. Some people who try to avoid pregnancy by using birth control find themselves pregnant anyway.

And what about pregnant teenagers? There are about 1.2 million teenage pregnancies each year. Almost forty percent choose abortion, about another twenty percent give their babies for adoption or miscarry, which means that about forty percent keep their babies. Such a large number of single, teenage mothers is a catastrophe for family life. Abortion is not necessarily an answer here, but so many children being raised in single-parent homes or by grandparents takes an immeasurable toll on mother, child, family, and society.

You can see that this topic is not easy. I cannot offer ten easy solutions on how to deal with the problem, something to laminate in plastic and carry in your wallet.

My time with the genetic counseling team moved me from a position of ease with abortion to seeing it as a necessary possibility but with very serious consequences. Only two things come easily to me now. One is the belief that abortion should not be used as contraception in gender selection, because nature has its own way of balancing genders that we ought not interrupt. And abortion for gender selection is sexist. The other is that abortion should not be used as contraception for convenience. The essence of pregnancy is stewardship, not convenience.

The preacher is again forthright concerning his own view.

I have come to believe that abortion is sometimes the better choice, in spite of its being undesirable, and that when we turn to it, we must throw ourselves on God's grace, knowing that medicine has given us divine-like power to see into the womb and to interrupt pregnancy but that no power on earth can give us divine wisdom to know unquestionably that what we do is right.

I think it is biblically right to believe that God is the first to suffer with us as we suffer in these agonizing situations. God does not abandon us, whatever the problems we face. God understands more than we how human and frail we are.

God stands with the couple who chooses to bear a child who they know will not live long. God stands with that child and those parents to strengthen them in whatever they must face. But God does not abandon the parents who stop a pregnancy. God, who knew the loss of his own son, does not turn away from parents who suffer the same anguish.

The preacher forthrightly states the promise of the gospel. This does not end the congregation's struggle with the issue, but assures them of God's continuing love and encouragement in the midst of struggle.

We do the best we can to be faithful to God. The way is not always easy nor is it always certain. But we do all we can humanly do when we take responsibility for our life's decisions, when we make them through prayer and the guidance of scripture and the use of wise counsel. God asks no more of us than that.

When our decisions seem, in time, not to be the best, then we are assured that God forgives.

And so the Psalmist cries,

> Search me, O God, and know my heart!
> Try me and know my thoughts!
> And see if there be any wicked way in me,
> and lead me in the way everlasting! (Ps. 139:23–24)

For parents weighing the awesome decision of whether to continue or end a pregnancy, for physicians, and nurses, and counselors, for those who live with the decision they have made in the past, that prayer of the Psalmist has never seemed more appropriate. May God keep us from easy judgments about the difficult decisions of others. And may God grant us peace with the decisions we make for ourselves and for our children. So may God lead us in the way everlasting.

The promises of God are good for all involved in the situation of abortion.

APPENDIXES

APPENDIX A
Earlier Discussions of Topical Preaching

The following are representative of earlier treatments of topical preaching: M. Reu, *Homiletics*, trans. Albert Steinhauser (1924; reprint, Grand Rapids: Baker Book House, 1967), pp. 425–430; Carl Patton, *The Preparation and Delivery of Sermons* (New York: Willett, Clark & Company, 1938), p. 124; John A. Broadus, *On the Preparation and Delivery of Sermons*, rev. ed., Jesse Weatherspoon (New York: Harper & Row Publishers, 1944), pp. 134–135; Andrew Blackwood, *The Preparation of Sermons* (New York: Abingdon-Cokesbury Press, 1948), pp. 101–108; H. Grady Davis, *Design for Preaching* (Philadelphia: Fortress Press, 1958), pp. 32–33; Richard Caemmerer, *Preaching for the Church* (St. Louis: Concordia Press, 1959), pp. 131–150; J. Daniel Bauman, *An Introduction to Contemporary Preaching* (Grand Rapids: Baker Book House, 1972), pp. 101–102; James Earl Massey, *Designing the Sermon* (Nashville: Abingdon Press, 1980), pp. 61–74.

The "life-situation sermon" was an especially influential mode of preaching and was often topical in approach. See especially Halford Luccock, *In the Minister's Workshop* (New York: Abingdon-Cokesbury Press, 1944), pp. 50–72; Charles F. Kemp, *Life Situation*

Preaching (St. Louis: Bethany Press, 1956); Edmund H. Linn, *Preaching as Counseling* (Valley Forge: Judson Press, 1966).

APPENDIX B
Literature on the Classification of Sermons

For representative attempts to classify sermons, see Andrew W. Blackwood, *The Preparation of Sermons* (Nashville: Abingdon Press, 1958), pp. 55–76, 101–108; H. Grady Davis, *Design for Preaching* (Philadelphia: Fortress Press, 1958), pp. 32–33, 48–49; C. S. Roddy, "The Classification of Sermons," in *Homiletics*, ed. Vernon Stanfield et al. (Grand Rapids: Baker Book House, 1967), pp. 31–43; J. Daniel Bauman, *An Introduction to Contemporary Preaching* (Grand Rapids: Baker Book House, 1972), pp. 101–104; John A. Broadus, *On the Preparation and Delivery of Sermons*, rev. ed., Vernon L. Stanfield (San Francisco: Harper & Row Publishers, 1979), pp. 54–76; James W. Cox, *Preaching* (San Francisco: Harper & Row Publishers, 1985), pp. 89–115, 129–160; Deane Kemper, *Effective Preaching* (Philadelphia: Westminster Press, 1985), pp. 55–57; Sidney Greidanus, *The Modern Preacher and the Ancient Text* (Grand Rapids: W. B. Eerdmans Publishing Co.; and Leicaster: Intervarsity Press, 1988), pp. 10–11.

More innovative (though not under the rubric of "classification") are Fred B. Craddock, *Preaching* (Nashville: Abingdon Press, 1985), esp. 171–175; David G. Buttrick, *Homiletic: Moves and Structures* (Philadelphia: Fortress Press, 1987), pp. 333–448; Thomas G. Long, *The Witness of Preaching* (Louisville: Westminster/John Knox Press, 1989), esp. pp. 80–84, 92–95.

APPENDIX C
Guides to Interpreting the Bible for Expository Preaching

Among the basic guides to interpreting the Bible for the expository sermon are O. C. Edwards, Jr., *The Living and Active Word* (New York: Seabury Press, 1975); Leander Keck, *The Bible in the Pulpit* (Nashville: Abingdon Press, 1978); William D. Thompson, *Preaching Biblically* (Nashville: Abingdon Press, 1980); Elizabeth

Achtemeier, *Creative Preaching* (Nashville: Abingdon Press, 1980); Reginald H. Fuller, *The Use of the Bible in Preaching* (Philadelphia: Fortress Press, 1981); O. C. Edwards, Jr., *Elements of Homiletic* (New York: Pueblo Press, 1982); John Hayes and Carl Holladay, *Biblical Exegesis* (Atlanta: John Knox Press, 1982); Gordon Fee, *New Testament Exegesis* (Philadelphia: Westminster Press, 1983); Ronald J. Allen, *Contemporary Biblical Interpretation for Preaching* (Valley Forge: Judson Press, 1984); Douglas Stuart, *Old Testament Exegesis*, rev. ed. (Philadelphia: Westminster Press, 1984); Fred B. Craddock, *Preaching* (Nashville: Abingdon Press, 1985), pp. 99–124; Richard C. White, *Biblical Preaching* (St. Louis: CBP Press, 1988); Ernest Best, *From Text to Sermon*, rev. ed. (Edinburgh: T & T Clark, 1988); Thomas G. Long, *The Witness of Preaching* (Louisville, Ky.: Westminster/John Knox Press, 1989), pp. 60–77.

Valuable expansions and correctives are exemplified by Justo and Catherine Gonzalez, *Liberation Preaching: The Pulpit and the Oppressed* (Nashville: Abingdon Press, 1980); Christopher Rowland and Mark Corner, *Liberating Exegesis* (Louisville, Ky.: Westminster/John Knox Press, 1989); Cain H. Felder, *Troubling Biblical Waters: Race, Class and Family* (Maryknoll, N.Y.: Orbis Books, 1989); Alice L. Laffey, *Introduction to the Old Testament: A Feminist Approach* (Philadelphia: Fortress Press, 1988).

APPENDIX D
Literature on Preaching on Social and Personal Issues

The standard homiletical guide to preaching in a social context is now *Preaching as a Social Act*, ed. Arthur Van Seters (Nashville: Abingdon Press, 1988). Other valuable works include Harold Bosley, *Preaching on Controversial Issues* (New York: Harper & Brothers, 1953); Otto J. Baab, *Prophetic Preaching: A New Approach* (Nashville: Abingdon Press, 1958); Roland Leavell, *Prophetic Preaching Then and Now* (Grand Rapids: Baker Book House, 1963); James Armstrong, *Telling the Truth: The Foolishness of Preaching in a Real World* (Waco: Word Books, 1977); Alvin C. Porteous, *Preaching to Suburban Captives* (Valley Forge: Judson Press, 1979); Justo and Catherine Gonzalez, *Liberation Preaching: The Pulpit and the Oppressed*

(Nashville: Abingdon Press, 1980); Dieter Hessel, *Social Ministry* (Philadelphia: Westminster Press, 1982), pp. 93–108; William Nottingham, *The Practice and Preaching of Liberation* (St. Louis: CBP Press, 1988); Ronald J. Sider and M. A. King, *Preaching about Life in a Threatening World* (Philadelphia: Westminster Press, 1987); William K. McElvaney, *Preaching from Camelot to Covenant: Announcing God's Action in the World* (Nashville: Abingdon Press, 1989).

Works that focus on bringing the gospel to bear on personal needs include Ronald E. Sleeth, *Proclaiming the Word* (Nashville: Abingdon Press, 1964), pp. 86–104; Edgar N. Jackson, *How to Preach to People's Needs* (Grand Rapids: Baker Book House, 1972); Harold T. Bryson and James C. Taylor, *Building Sermons to Meet People's Needs* (Nashville: Broadman Press, 1980); David K. Switzer, *Pastor, Preacher, Person* (Nashville; Abingdon Press, 1979); two series of articles by Wayne E. Oates, which appeared in *Preaching:* "Preaching and Pastoral Care," 1/3 (1985), pp. 3–5; "Preaching to Marriage and Family Needs" 1/4 (1986), pp. 13–15; "Preaching to Emotional Needs" 1/5 (1986), pp. 5–7; "Preaching and Grief" 1/6 (1986), pp. 4–6; "Preaching to Meet Crisis Needs" 2/1 (1986), pp. 3–5; and "The Presence of God in the Heart of Preaching" 2/4 (1987), pp. 27–29; "The Presence of God in the Heart of Preaching (Part Two)" 2/5 (1987), pp. 29–30; "The Presence of God as Stranger in the Preaching Event" 2/6 (1987), pp. 31–33; "The 'Dark Side' of the Presence of God in Preaching" 3/1 (1987), pp. 25–27; Elizabeth Achtemeier, *Preaching About Family Relationships* (Philadelphia: Westminster Press, 1987); David H. C. Read, *Preaching About the Needs of Real People* (Philadelphia: Westminster Press, 1988).

APPENDIX E
Literature on Preaching on Christian Doctrine

The best book on doctrinal preaching is William J. Carl, *Preaching Christian Doctrine* (Philadelphia: Fortress Press, 1984). Other standard works include W. E. Sangster, *Doctrinal Preaching: Its Neglect and Recovery* (Birmingham, England: Berean Press, 1953); Eric Baker, *Preaching Theology* (London: Epworth Press, 1954); Andrew W. Blackwood, *Doctrinal Preaching for Today* (Nashville: Abingdon

Press, 1956); Merrill R. Abbey, *Living Doctrine in a Vital Pulpit* (Nashville: Abingdon Press, 1964); Ronald E. Sleeth, *Proclaiming the Word* (Nashville: Abingdon Press, 1964), pp. 66–85.

APPENDIX F
Helps in Biblical Interpretation

Among the better Bible dictionaries are: *The Interpreter's Dictionary of the Bible*, ed. George A. Buttrick et al. (1964; reprint, Nashville: Abingdon Press, 1976), 5 vols.; *The International Standard Bible Encyclopedia*, rev. ed., ed. Geoffrey W. Bromily (Grand Rapids: W. B. Eerdmans Publishing Co., 1979–1988), 4 vols.; *Harper's Bible Dictionary*, ed. Paul J. Achtemeier (San Francisco: Harper & Row Publishers, 1985); *Theological Dictionary of the Old Testament*, ed. G. J. Botterweck and H. Ringgrenn, trans. by John T. Willis and David E. Green (Grand Rapids: W. B. Eerdmans Publishing Co., 1974–1990), 6 vols.; *The Dictionary of Bible and Religion*, ed. William H. Gentz (Nashville: Abingdon Press, 1986); *Exegetical Dictionary of the New Testament*, ed. Horst R. Balz and Gerhard Schneider, trans. Virgil P. Howard and James W. Thompson (Grand Rapids: W. B. Eerdmans Publishing Co., 1990ff.), 3 vols.

Especially valuable on Judaism from the world of antiquity to today is *Encyclopedia Judaica*, ed. Cecil Roth (New York: Macmillan Co., 1972), 16 vols. A fascinating work on biblical scholarship is *A Dictionary of Biblical Interpretation*, ed. R. J. Coggins and J. L. Houlden (London: SCM Press; and Philadelphia: Trinity Press International, 1990). *The Theological Dictionary of the New Testament*, ed. Gerhard Kittel and Gerhard Friedrich, trans. Geoffrey W. Bromiley (Grand Rapids: W. B. Eerdmans Publishing Co., 1964–1976), 10 vols., can still be used cautiously.

APPENDIX G
Standard Theological Reference Works

On church history: *The Westminster Dictionary of Church History*, ed. Jerald C. Brauer (Philadelphia: Westminster Press, 1971); *The Oxford Dictionary of the History of the Christian Church*, 2d ed., ed. F. L. Cross and E. A. Livingstone (London: Oxford University

Press, 1974); *Eerdmans Handbook to the History of Christianity*, ed. Tim Dowley (Grand Rapids: W. B. Eerdmans Publishing Co., 1977).

On theology and theologians: *The Encyclopedia of Theology: The Concise Sacramentum Mundi*, ed. Karl Rahner (New York: Seabury Press, 1975); *Eerdmans Handbook to Christian Belief*, ed. Robin Keeley (Grand Rapids: W. B. Eerdmans Publishing Co., 1982); *The Westminster Dictionary of Christian Theology*, ed. Alan Richardson and John Bowden (Philadelphia: Westminster Press, 1983); *A Handbook of Christian Theologians*, ed. Martin E. Marty and Dean G. Peerman (Nashville: Abingdon Press, 1984); *Evangelical Dictionary of Theology*, ed. Walter A. Elwell (Grand Rapids: Baker Book House, 1989); John Bowden, *A Concise Dictionary of Theology* (Philadelphia: Trinity Press International, 1990); John Bowden, *Who's Who in Theology* (Philadelphia: Trinity Press International, 1991).

On world religions: *The Perennial Dictionary of World Religions*, ed. Keith Crim (San Francisco: Harper & Row Publishers, 1989).

On miscellaneous topics: *The Westminster Dictionary of Liturgy and Worship*, ed. J. G. Davies (Philadelphia: Westminster Press, 1986); *The Westminster Dictionary of Christian Ethics*, ed. John F. Childress and John MacQuarrie (Philadelphia: Westminster Press, 1986); *The Westminster Dictionary of Spirituality*, ed. Gordon S. Wakefield (Philadelphia: Westminster Press, 1983); *Dictionary of Pastoral Care and Counseling*, ed. Rodney J. Hunter (Nashville: Abingdon Press, 1990); *Dictionary of the Ecumenical Movement*, ed. Geoffrey Wainwright (Grand Rapids: W. B. Eerdmans Publishing Co., 1991).

An excellent cross-cultural work is *The Encyclopedia of Religion*, ed. Mircea Eliade (New York: Macmillan Co., 1987), 16 vols. An excellent resource for placing topics in philosophical discussion is *The Encyclopedia of Philosophy*, ed. Paul Edwards (New York: Macmillan Co., 1967).

APPENDIX H
Guides to Contemporary Theology

The following help orient the reader to the various streams in contemporary theology. One of the most complete guides is *The Mod-*

ern Theologians, ed. David F. Ford (London: Basil Blackwell Ltd., 1989), 2 vols. Other useful studies include David Tracy, *Blessed Rage for Order* (New York: Seabury Press, 1975); Gayraud S. Wilmore and James H. Cone, *Black Theology: A Documentary History 1966–1979* (Maryknoll, N.Y.: Orbis Books, 1979); Lonnie Kliever, *The Shattered Spectrum of Contemporary Theology* (Atlanta: John Knox Press, 1981); Deane William Ferm, *Contemporary American Theologies: A Critical Survey* (New York: Seabury Press, 1981); William A. Placher, *Unapologetic Theology* (Louisville, Ky.: Westminster/John Knox Press, 1989); Justo L. Gonzalez, *Christian Thought Revisited: Three Types of Theology* (Nashville: Abingdon Press, 1989); John MacQuarrie, *Twentieth Century Religious Thought* (Philadelphia: Trinity Press International, 1989); *Christian Theology: An Introduction to Its Traditions and Tasks,* rev. ed., ed. Peter C. Hodgson and Robert H. King (Philadelphia: Fortress Press, 1985).

For surveys of theology outside of Europe and North America, see *Theology in the Americas,* ed. Sergio Torres and John Eagleson (Maryknoll, N.Y.: Orbis Books, 1976); and *Third World Theologies,* ed. K. C. Abraham (Maryknoll, N.Y.: Orbis Books, 1990).

NOTES

INTRODUCTION

1. Some writers point to the possibility of topical preaching but do not develop a detailed strategy for it; see Deane Kemper, *Effective Preaching* (Philadelphia: Westminster Press, 1985), pp. 30–32; James Cox, *Preaching* (San Francisco: Harper & Row Publishers, 1985), p. 103. Other widely used textbooks give little attention to topical preaching as such, e.g., John Killinger, *Fundamentals of Preaching* (Philadelphia: Fortress Press, 1985); Fred B. Craddock, *Preaching* (Nashville: Abingdon Press, 1985); Thomas G. Long, *The Witness of Preaching* (Louisville: Westminster/John Knox Press, 1989).

2. David G. Buttrick, *Homiletic: Moves and Structures* (Philadelphia: Fortress Press, 1987), pp. 405–448.

CHAPTER ONE
Locating the Topical Sermon on the Homiletical Map

1. Developing methods and norms for critical evaluation of all aspects of ministerial practice is a leading theme of the current movement in practical theology, e.g., Don S. Browning, ed., *Practical Theology* (San Francisco: Harper & Row Publishers, 1983); Don S. Browning, David Polk, and Ian S. Evison, eds., *The Education of*

the Practical Theologian (Atlanta: Scholars Press, 1989). The present essay is not a fully developed exploration in the new paradigm of practical theology but does seek to incorporate some of its concerns.

2. I deal with these claims about the Bible in "Theological Method in Biblical Interpretation for Preaching," in Clark M. Williamson and Ronald J. Allen's *A Credible and Timely Word* (St. Louis: Chalice Press, 1991). Even when a text is problematic, it is nearly always profitable for a congregation to engage the text. An unhealthy text can be the starting point for a very healthy conversation.

3. David G. Buttrick, *Homiletic: Moves and Structures* (Philadelphia: Fortress Press, 1987), p. 421. On the interrelationship of self and society, see Catherine Keller, *From a Broken Web: Separation, Sexism, Self* (Boston: Beacon Press, 1986).

4. This formulation of the gospel is drawn from my colleague, Clark M. Williamson.

5. Buttrick, *Homiletic*, p. 417.

6. Ibid., p. 416.

7. Ronald E. Sleeth, *Proclaiming the Word* (Nashville: Abingdon Press, 1964), p. 24.

8. Ibid., p. 37.

9. The classic discussion of logic and movement in sermons is Fred B. Craddock, *As One Without Authority*, 3d ed. (1971; reprint, Nashville: Abingdon Press, 1979). Cf. his *Preaching* (Nashville: Abingdon Press, 1985), pp. 170–193. On inductive and deductive patterns of reasoning, see James B. Conant, *Two Modes of Thought* (New York: Trident Press, 1964), and Stephen Toulmin, *The Uses of Argument* (Oxford: Cambridge University Press, 1958), pp. 118–123, 147–148.

10. Craddock, *As One Without Authority*, p. 57; Locke Bowman, Jr., *Straight Talk About Teaching in Today's Church* (Philadelphia: Westminster Press, 1968), p. 38.

11. Craddock, *As One Without Authority*, p. 57, and Bowman, p. 33.

12. This is true of the several significant movements and authors in contemporary homiletics. See the descriptions and evaluations in Richard Eslinger, *A New Hearing* (Nashville: Abingdon

Press, 1987). To Eslinger's catalogue we should now add Thomas H. Troeger, *Imagining the Sermon* (Nashville: Abingdon Press, 1990).

13. Craddock, *As One Without Authority*, p. 57.

14. Ibid.

CHAPTER TWO
Occasions for the Topical Sermon

1. David G. Buttrick, *Homiletic: Moves and Structures* (Philadelphia: Fortress Press, 1987), p. 409.

2. Clifford Geertz, *The Interpretation of Cultures* (New York: Basic Books, 1973), pp. 87–125.

3. Buttrick, p. 410.

4. Fred B. Craddock, "Preaching and the Rhetoric of Excess" (lecture), Candler School of Theology Ministers' Week (1991), Emory University, Atlanta, Ga.

5. On critical correlation, see Paul Tillich, *Systematic Theology* vol. 1 (Chicago: University of Chicago Press, 1951), pp. 59–66. David Tracy offers important revisions to Tillich's approach in *Blessed Rage for Order: The New Pluralism in Theology* (New York: Seabury Press, 1975) and *The Analogical Imagination: Christian Theology and the Culture of Pluralism* (New York: Crossroad, 1981). A widely read text that shows how doctrine has evolved in response to changing questions and worldviews is *Christian Theology: An Introduction to Its Traditions and Tasks*, ed. Peter C. Hodgson and Robert H. King, rev. ed. (Philadelphia: Fortress Press, 1985).

6. E. Brooks Holifield, "Text and Pretext in American Preaching" (lecture), Candler School of Theology Ministers' Week (1991), Emory University, Atlanta, Ga.

7. Paul R. Debenport, "Guess Who's Invited to Dinner," *Journal for Preachers* 12/3 (1989), pp. 53–56.

8. Ibid., p. 54. The phrase "more caring than careful" is cited by Debenport from William Willimon, "Sunday Dinner: The Lord's Supper and the Christian Life," *The Upper Room* (1981), p. 45.

9. E. P. Sanders, *Jesus and Judaism* (Philadelphia: Fortress Press, 1985), pp. 174–211.

10. For an approach to the rapidly changing AIDS phenomenon, see Ronald Sunderland and Earl Shelp, *Handle With Care: A Handbook for Care Teams Serving People with AIDS* (Nashville: Abingdon Press, 1990).

11. Sandra M. Schneiders, "Does the Bible Have a Postmodern Message," in *Postmodern Theology*, ed. Frederic B. Burnham (San Francisco: Harper & Row Publishers, 1989), p. 64.

12. E.g., Lynn White, "The Historical Roots of Our Ecologic Crisis," *Science* 155 (1967), pp. 1203–1207.

13. E.g., Walter Brueggemann, *Genesis*, Interpretation Commentary (Atlanta: John Knox Press, 1982), pp. 32–33.

14. Schneiders, p. 65.

15. As reported in conversation by Clark M. Williamson in conjunction with the preparation of Clark M. Williamson and Ronald J. Allen, *Interpreting Difficult Texts: Anti-Judaism and Christian Preaching* (London: SCM Press; and Philadelphia: Trinity Press International, 1989), pp. 9–27.

16. Ibid., pp. 28–55.

17. Ibid., p. 2.

18. Cf. my "Preaching Against the Text," *Encounter* 48 (1987), pp. 105–116; and Clark M. Williamson and Ronald J. Allen's *A Credible and Timely Word* (St. Louis: Chalice Press, 1991), chap. 4.

19. This idea was inspired by my colleague Keith Watkins, in his *Faithful and Fair: Transcending Sexist Language in Worship* (Nashville: Abingdon Press, 1981), pp. 67–68.

CHAPTER THREE
Preparing the Topical Sermon

1. Seasoned preachers typically report to me that discipline in preparation actually increases their sense of freedom to be creative in developing the content and style of the sermon.

2. David G. Buttrick, *Homiletic: Moves and Structures* (Philadelphia: Fortress Press, 1987), p. 425. At times, these criteria overlap.

3. Ibid.

4. One of Walter Brueggemann's many discussions of this phenomenon is especially concise: "The Social Nature of the Biblical

Text," in *Preaching as a Social Act,* ed. Arthur Van Seters (Nashville: Abingdon Press, 1989), pp. 127–165, esp. 134–150.

5. E.g., Hans-Georg Gadamer, *Truth and Method*, trans. Garrett Barden and John Cumming (New York: Seabury Press, 1975), pp. 323–324, 357–366.

6. Among the better concordances are Clinton Morrison, *An Analytical Concordance to the Revised Standard Version of the New Testament* (Philadelphia: Westminster Press, 1979); Richard E. Whitaker, *The Eerdmans Analytical Concordance to the Revised Standard Version of the Bible* (Grand Rapids: W. B. Eerdmans Publishing Co., 1988).

7. On the gospel as the highest authority in the church, see Clark M. Williamson and Ronald J. Allen, *The Teaching Minister* (Louisville, Ky.: Westminster/John Knox Press, 1991), pp. 65–82; and Richard K. Osmer, *A Teachable Spirit* (Louisville, Ky.: Westminster/John Knox Press, 1990), pp. 90–98, 175–181.

8. Douglas John Hall, *The Steward: A Biblical Symbol Come of Age* (New York: Friendship Press, 1982), pp. 30–41.

9. Douglas John Hall, *Christian Mission: The Stewardship of Life in the Kingdom of Death* (New York: Friendship Press, 1985).

10. E.g., I. Carter Heyward, *Our Passion for Justice: Images of Power, Sexuality and Liberation* (New York: Pilgrim Press, 1984), and idem, *Speaking of Christ: A Lesbian Feminist Voice* (New York: Pilgrim Press, 1989).

11. *The Book of Discipline of the United Methodist Church*, 1988 (Nashville: United Methodist Publishing House, 1988).

12. A work which helps congregations discover their own identity and history through self-analysis is James Hopewell's *Congregation* (Philadelphia: Fortress Press, 1987). Cf. the methods in congregational study in Jackson W. Carroll, Carl S. Dudley, and William McKinney, *Handbook for Congregational Studies* (Nashville: Abingdon Press, 1986). Also useful is Joe Holland and Peter Henriot, *Social Analysis: Linking Faith and Justice*, rev. ed. (Maryknoll, N.Y.: Orbis Books, 1983). For homiletical implications, see Don M. Wardlaw, "Preaching as the Interface of Two Social Worlds: The Congregation as Corporate Agent in the Act of Preaching" in *Preaching as a Social Act*, pp. 55–94.

13. On the importance of imagination in preaching, pivotal works are Charles L. Rice, *Interpretation and Imagination* (Philadelphia: Fortress Press, 1970); Fred B. Craddock, *As One Without Authority,* 3d ed. (1971; reprint, Nashville: Abingdon Press, 1979), pp. 77–97; Paul Scott Wilson, *The Imagination of the Heart* (Nashville: Abingdon Press, 1988); *Learning Preaching,* ed. Don M. Wardlaw (Lincoln, Ill.: Lincoln College and Seminary Press for the Academy of Homiletics, 1989), pp. 75–81; and Thomas H. Troeger, *Imagining the Sermon* (Nashville: Abingdon Press, 1990).

14. These criteria are developed in Clark M. Williamson and Ronald J. Allen, *The Teaching Minister* (Louisville, Ky.: Westminster/John Knox Press, 1991), pp. 75–81; idem, *A Credible and Timely Word* (St. Louis: Chalice Press, 1991), chap. 4; and from Clark M. Williamson, "Preaching the Gospel: Some Theological Reflections," *Encounter* 49 (1988), pp. 191–198. The criteria are adapted from James A. Sanders, *Canon and Community* (Philadelphia: Fortress Press, 1984), and Schubert M. Ogden, *The Point of Christology* (San Francisco: Harper & Row Publishers, 1982), pp. 89–96. These simple criteria do not exhaust all considerations that must be taken into account in moral decisions. See also Edward L. Long, *A Survey of Recent Christian Ethics* (New York: Oxford University Press, 1982), and the magisterial work by James M. Gustafson, *Ethics from a Theocentric Perspective* (1981; reprint, Chicago: University of Chicago Press, 1984), 2 vols.

15. Buttrick, p. 417.

16. See Ronald J. Allen, *Preaching for Growth* (St. Louis: CBP Press, 1988), pp. 31–34. Some authors in the field of homiletics think that this statement is not so much a hard proposition as it is a softer focus statement. I lean toward the former. For an elegant statement of the latter, see Eugene L. Lowry, *How to Preach a Parable: Design for Narrative Sermons* (Nashville: Abingdon Press, 1989), p. 35. Representatives of the whole spectrum share a desire for the sermon to be a unified piece. On unity, see Craddock, *Preaching,* pp. 155–157.

17. Allen, *Preaching for Growth,* pp. 9–15, 17–20.

18. Two penetrating exposés of moralism and its problems are Leander Keck, *The Bible in the Pulpit* (Nashville: Abingdon Press,

1978), pp. 100–104; and D. Newell Williams, "Disciples Piety: A Historical Review with Implications for Spiritual Formation," *Encounter* 47 (1986), pp. 13–17.

19. Harold Bosley, *Preaching on Controversial Issues* (New York: Harper & Brothers, 1953), pp. 21–22. Cf. Ronald E. Sleeth, *Proclaiming the Word* (Nashville: Abingdon Press, 1964), pp. 107–117.

20. Fred B. Craddock, *Overhearing the Gospel: Preaching and Teaching the Faith to Persons Who Have Already Heard* (Nashville: Abingdon Press, 1978), pp. 101–119.

21. Ibid., p. 103.

22. Ibid., p. 137.

23. Ibid., p. 131.

24. Ibid., p. 138.

CHAPTER FOUR
Some Forms for the Topical Sermon

1. On sermon form, see Fred B. Craddock, *Preaching* (Nashville: Abingdon Press, 1985), pp. 170–209.

2. Thomas G. Long, *The Witness of Preaching* (Louisville, Ky.: Westminster/John Knox Press, 1989), pp. 133–147. Cf. David G. Buttrick, *Homiletic: Moves and Structures* (Philadelphia: Fortress Press, 1987), pp. 83–96.

3. See Buttrick, pp. 97–109.

4. On the "quadrilateral" see Max L. Stackhouse, *Public Theology and Political Economy* (Grand Rapids: W. B. Eerdmans Publishing Co., 1987), pp. 1–16.

5. I use the word *experience* here in a more general way than it is usually used in reference to the quadrilateral.

6. Don S. Browning, *Religious Ethics and Pastoral Care* (Philadelphia: Fortress Press, 1983), pp. 51–52, 99–118.

7. Browning does not discuss the criteria of appropriateness, intelligibility, and moral plausibility.

8. Persons with the following characteristics can usually withstand direct confrontation: "a relatively well-differentiated personality, a reasonably strong sense of self, a fairly intact superego, and a reasonably accurate perceptual or ego capacity" (Browning,

p. 118). To the degree that a congregation has a "personality," the preacher might use the presence of such qualities as a guide to help determine the tone of the sermon.

9. Fred B. Craddock, *As One Without Authority*, 3d ed. (Nashville: Abingdon Press, 1979), pp. 51–118. For an assessment of Craddock's general approach see Richard Eslinger, *A New Hearing: Living Options in Homiletic Method* (Nashville: Abingdon Press, 1987), pp. 122–126.

10. Ibid., p. 125.

11. See above, p. 12.

12. Buttrick, *Homiletic*, pp. 405–426. For an assessment of Buttrick's general approach, see Eslinger, pp. 159–160.

13. On plot, see Buttrick, pp. 285–332.

14. On moves, see ibid., pp. 23–82.

15. This example is adapted from ibid., p. 430.

16. Ibid., p. 84.

17. The distinction between personal and social is really only a matter of emphasis since self and society are inextricably intertwined (Buttrick, p. 423).

18. As formulated by G. Edwin Osborn, "Basic Principles of Homiletics," unpublished manuscript (Enid, Okla.: Phillips University, 1945), who calls it a psychological approach to preaching.

19. Craddock, *As One Without Authority*, pp. 147–48.

20. I mention seven other homiletical approaches. Although developed for biblical preaching, they can easily be adapted to topical preaching. (a) Milton Crum's three-part sermon form in his *Manual on Preaching* (Valley Forge: Judson Press, 1977). (b) Sermon as moving like a short story in Edmund Steimle, Morris Niedenthal, and Charles Rice's *Preaching the Story* (Philadelphia: Fortress Press, 1980). For assessment, see Eslinger, pp. 28–32. (c) Eugene L. Lowry's five-phase sermonic plot in his *The Homiletical Plot* (Atlanta: John Knox Press, 1980). For assessment see Eslinger, pp. 84–89. Cf. Lowry's *How to Preach a Parable: Designs for Narrative Sermons* (Nashville: Abingdon Press, 1989). (d) Henry H. Mitchell's narrative, character sketch, group study, and metaphor in his *Celebration and Experience in Preaching* (Nashville: Abingdon Press, 1990). (e) Thomas H. Troeger's sermon as moving images in his *Imagining the Sermon* (Nashville: Abingdon Press, 1990), pp. 39–

47. (f) Sermon as single narrative in David M. Brown, *Dramatic Narrative in Preaching* (Valley Forge: Judson Press, 1981). (g) The "hourglass" model outlined on p. 17. For other structural possibilities, see Long, pp. 126–129; and Craddock, *Preaching*, p. 176.

CHAPTER FIVE
Strategies for Preaching on Controversial Topics

1. These strategies are similar to those found in other works. Note the literature cited in Appendix D. Our approaches are also sympathetic to those made by researchers in persuasive speech, such as Ruth A. Clark, *Persuasive Messages* (New York: Harper & Row Publishers, 1984).

2. Bonita L. Benda, "The Silence Is Broken: Preaching on Social Justice Issues" (Th.D. diss., Iliff School of Theology, 1983), pp. 251–252. Cf. Kenneth Burke, *A Rhetoric of Motives* (New York: Prentice Hall, 1950), pp. 55–59.

3. Benda, pp. 274–275 (where voluminous literature is cited). Cf. Hans Van der Geest, *Presence in the Pulpit: The Impact of Personality in Preaching*, trans. Douglas W. Stott (Atlanta: John Knox Press, 1981), pp. 31–68, 143–151.

4. Van der Geest, pp. 71–74; Benda, pp. 299–300.

5. Walter Brueggemann, *The Prophetic Imagination* (Philadelphia: Fortress Press, 1978), p. 24.

6. David G. Buttrick, *Homiletic: Moves and Structures* (Philadelphia: Fortress Press, 1987), p. 123.

7. George Lakhoff and Mark Johnson, *Metaphors We Live By* (Chicago: University of Chicago Press, 1980).

8. Fred B. Craddock, *As One Without Authority*, 3d ed. (Nashville: Abingdon Press, 1979), p. 78. On images, see pp. 77–97. Idem, *Overhearing the Gospel: Preaching and Teaching the Faith to Persons Who Have Already Heard* (Nashville: Abingdon Press, 1978), pp. 125–140. Cf. Van der Geest, pp. 135–138; Clark, p. 208; Thomas H. Troeger, "The Social Power of Myth as a Key to Preaching on Social Issues," in *Preaching as a Social Act*, ed. Arthur Van Seters (Nashville: Abingdon Press, 1989), pp. 205–234; and Walter Brueggemann, *Finally Comes the Poet: Daring Speech for Proclamation* (Minneapolis: Fortress Press, 1990).

9. Craddock, *As One Without Authority*, pp. 92–96.

10. Van der Geest, p. 130.

11. Benda, p. 300; cf. pp. 267–270. On telling stories see Charles L. Rice, *Interpretation and Imagination* (Philadelphia: Fortress Press, 1970), pp. 66–74, 86–109; Peter M. Morgan, *Storyweaving: Using Stories to Transform Your Congregation* (St. Louis: CBP Press, 1986); and Ruth E. Sawyer, *The Way of the Storyteller* (New York: Viking Press, 1965). Thomas E. Boomershine's *Story Journey: An Invitation to the Gospel as Storytelling* (Nashville: Abingdon Press, 1988) is the definitive work on biblical storytelling.

12. An interviewee cited in Benda, p. 305. Cf. Clark, p. 73.

13. Benda, pp. 257, 265–266. Van der Geest notes that listeners especially value the preacher's competence in the subject area of the sermon (p. 143).

14. Kenneth I. Pargament and Donald V. DeRosa, "What Was That Sermon About? Predicting Memory for Religious Messages from Cognitive Psychology Theory," *Journal for the Scientific Study of Religion* 24 (1985), p. 192.

15. Benda, p. 279.

16. Ibid., p. 280.

17. Van der Geest, pp. 113–114.

18. Benda, pp. 292–294. This is stressed by Clark, pp. 197–203.

19. Kimball Boyd Coburn, "Prophetic Preaching from a Pastoral Base" (D.Min. thesis, School of Theology at Claremont, 1975), p. 43.

20. Roger D. Fallot, "When Congregations Won't Listen," *The Christian Ministry* 16 (March, 1985), p. 15.

21. Ibid., pp. 15–16.

22. Note Craddock, *As One Without Authority*, p. 78.

23. Coburn, p. 43.

24. Fallot, p. 16. Clark, p. 37, notes that a particular speech sometimes has an "intermediate" character. Of course, there are times when a situation is so desperate that the preacher must ask the congregation to make quantum leaps in thought and action.

25. Van der Geest, p. 121.

26. Benda, p. 294.

27. Van der Geest, p. 122. Cf. pp. 115–117.

28. Benda, p. 302.

29. Kelly Miller Smith, *Social Crisis Preaching* (Macon, Ga.: Mercer University Press, 1984), p. 83.

30. Bosley, p. 22. Cf. Craddock, *As One Without Authority,* p. 91.

31. Van der Geest, pp. 40–50. For guidance on delivery see Charles L. Bartow, *The Preaching Moment* (Nashville: Abingdon, 1980); and idem, *Effective Speech Communication in Leading Worship* (Nashville: Abingdon Press, 1988); *Learning Preaching,* ed. Don M. Wardlaw (Lincoln, Ill.: Lincoln College and Seminary Press for the Academy of Homiletics, 1989), pp. 160–166.

32. Benda, pp. 290–291.

33. Brueggemann, *The Prophetic Imagination,* p. 50. Cf. Gregory Baum, "Resistance to Prophetic Preaching," *Arc* 14, no. 2 (1987), pp. 47–53.

34. On the multiple purposes of feedback see D. J. Cowley, *Understanding Communications: The Signifying Web* (New York: Gordon & Breach Science Publishers, 1982), esp. pp. 3–11, 58–65; and Don Jackson, "The Function of Feedback in Preaching," *The Journal of Communication and Religion* 14/1 (1991), pp. 40–47.

35. As implied in the comments in Benda, pp. 288–289.

36. On the congregation as a system, see chap. 3, n. 17.

37. Pargament and DeRosa, p. 190.

38. Ibid., p. 180.

CHAPTER SIX
Sample Topical Sermons

1. "Forgiveness," *The Oxford English Dictionary* (Oxford: Clarendon Press, 1933), pp. 452–453.

2. Brian Childs, "Forgiveness," *Dictionary of Pastoral Care,* ed. Rodney J. Hunter (Nashville: Abingdon Press, 1990), p. 439.

3. These steps are simplified from David Augsburger, *Caring Enough to Forgive* (Scottdale, Pa.: Herald Press, 1981).

4. Ibid., p. 15.

5. Lewis B. Smedes, *Forgive and Forget* (San Francisco: Harper & Row Publishers, 1984), p. 108.

6. Karl Barth, *Church Dogmatics,* trans. G. T. Thompson and Harold Knight, ed. G. W. Bromiley and T. F. Torrance (Edinburgh: T & T Clark Co., 1956), vol. I/2, pp. 61–67.

7. Paul Tillich, *Systematic Theology*, vol. III (Chicago: University of Chicago Press, 1963), pp. 152–155.

8. Søren Kierkegaard, *The Works of Love*, trans. H. Hong and E. Hong (New York: Harper & Row Publishers, 1964), pp. 22–23.

9. Lawrence J. Hatterer, *Changing Homosexuality in the Male* (New York: McGraw-Hill Publishing Co., 1970), pp. 34–42.

10. Quoted by Letha Scanzoni, "Conservative Christians and Gay Civil Rights," *The Christian Century* 92 (1976), p. 861.

11. Report of the United Presbyterian Task Force to Study Homosexuality (mimeographed ed., January 23, 1978), p. 109.

12. William Barnwell, "Personal Perspective," *The Christian Century* 95 (1978), pp. 29–30.

13. The General Assembly of the Presbyterian Church (U.S.A.), "The Covenant of Life and the Caring Community, and Covenant and Creation: Theological Reflections on Contraception and Abortion" (1983; repr. Louisville, Ky.: Office of the General Assembly, 1988), p. 47.

14. John Calvin, *Institutes of the Christian Religion*, ed. John T. McNeill, trans. by Ford L. Battles (Philadelphia: Westminster Press, 1950), I.17.4, p. 216.

15. "The Covenant of Life and the Caring Community, and Covenant and Creation," p. 24.